JUST

A LITTLE

BUZZED

TAIRA SOO

Published by split & type

Printed in the United States of America

First Edition

Cover Design and Interior Formatting by Nuno Moreira, NM DESIGN

ISBN Paperback: 979-8-9995465-0-0

ISBN eBook: 979-8-9995465-1-7

split & type

JUST

A LITTLE

BUZZED

A LIFE TOLD SIDEWAYS

TAIRA SOO

For the universe—
who whispered, then shouted,
then kicked down the door.

I heard you. I'm writing.

before the buzz
(real talk before the real story)

This isn't a manual.
Not tied in a bow or built for takeaways.
It's what spilled out after everything cracked, then got rebuilt.

A detour through the sharp left turns life never warns you about:
Illness. Identity. Endings. Beginnings.

I buzzed my hair. Burned the playbook. Let go of what wasn't real.
Kept the humor. Took the wisdom. Still here.

Before the spotlight, before the crash-and-comebacks—I was the kid
in the back row, whispering *not me*, hoping no one would notice.

I didn't come out swinging.
I shapeshifted.
Stumbled. Performed. Disappeared.
Became.

This is a true story.
Blurry in places. Sharp in others.

No hero arc. No filter.
Some names have been changed.
Some scenes reconstructed—for clarity, not fiction.

I didn't plan to write this.
But the whispers got loud enough to drown everything else out.

So here we are—
Me, finally saying it.
You, reading it.

What you'll find: glitter and scars.
Cringe and grace.
Some near-breakdowns. Hard-won light.
Maybe even something that makes you laugh, flinch, or feel a little less alone.

It's not polished. But it's real.
It beats with heart.

Just so we're clear—
Reinvention is always on the table.
Even if you're off-script.
Even if your hair's falling out.
Even if the room goes quiet and no one claps.

You can still start over.
You can still call it a comeback—
Even if no one saw the fall.

Thanks for being here.
The next chapter's waiting.

✦

With love—and a wink,
Taira

introduction

I'm not famous.
So why write a memoir?

Because I have something to say—
and I finally stopped waiting to say it.

Someone once told me—a fortune teller, a mystic, or maybe just a
very intense barista with a crescent moon tattoo and unsettling eye
contact—that I was here to help people.
That telling my story was part of it.
Writing a book even came up.

I smiled, nodded, ordered my oat milk latte, and kept it moving.

Then—boom. The stars aligned.
Or maybe it was the Lion's Mane talking.

I started taking mushrooms—the legal, brain-boosting kind.
(Not opposed to the trippy kind either.)
I thought they'd help my memory.
Instead, they cracked something open.

Now here I am.
Writing this.
Wondering if that barista-mystic was right.

My gut doesn't miss.
When I follow it, things click.
When I don't? Chaos.

So I'm following the hum.
That itch. That nudge.
That shove I couldn't ignore.

Not here to change the world—
but maybe it'll help someone feel less alone in theirs.
Or laugh. Or cry. Or say, *Same.*

This isn't a TED Talk.
Not a step-by-step for surviving life.
It's a messy, honest ride through the things that broke me—and the
things that built me.
Scattered moments that somehow hold the whole story.

I've been loud. Lost. Burned out. Broken. Rebuilt.
And I'm here.

Writing this made me dig through the blur, the cringe—
and weirdly, I loved it.

Here's what I do know:
I love my life. I love what I do.
I get to make things on my own terms.

For a while, I found a rhythm.
Stopped hustling for crumbs.
Trusted my voice. Protected my peace.

Things were good.

And then—cancer.

When I finally felt at home in my skin,
my body issued an eviction notice.

No warning. No appeal. Just: *Get out.*

That wasn't the plan.
But neither were most of the things that shaped me.

That's the thing about life:
You screw up. You pivot.
You claw your way forward.

You laugh when you can.
Cry when you must.
And keep going.

That's why I'm writing this.
Not because I had it all figured out—
but because I finally said *yes*.

Maybe that barista had a point.
Maybe we all need a little magic, (*and caffeine*) to begin.
Or maybe we need to stop stalling—
take a breath—
and *go*.

✦

bologna hour

The smallest moments stay loud the longest.

survival was the first act

The lights were blinding.
The crowd, electric.
Somewhere between the roar and the rhythm, I caught myself midair—
right in it.

Buzzed head. Locked eyes. Spirit lit.
Baptized in light. Wired to the beat.

I'd danced on stages I used to dream about—
award shows and stadiums that once felt mythic.

Bookings. Rehearsals. Fittings.
Another city. Another stage.
Always the sparkle—never the story.

Amsterdam one night. London the next.
No sleep. Just lashes and luggage.

Green rooms full of Red Bull and razor-edge nerves.
The twitchy hum before the cue.

Pure electricity.
We weren't famous. But we were there.
In the eye of the storm. The thick of the moment.

But that kind of presence?
It doesn't start on stage.

✦

Fifth grade. English class. First period after lunch—when survival
meant strategy.

Some kids were half-asleep, faces pressed to their desks.
Others were wired from Capri Suns, trading snacks like mini
stockbrokers.

I sat with my feet tucked under my chair.
My stomach churned.
Bologna on white bread, cut in half and wrapped in foil. No crusts.
Mom always took them off, even when I said I didn't care anymore.

The classroom smelled like Elmer's glue, pencil shavings, and
something burnt—maybe spaghetti sauce, maybe mystery meat.
Whatever it was, it lingered like a bad decision.

The hum of fluorescent lights droned overhead.
The walls were plastered with motivational posters no one read.
"Be the reason someone smiles today."
Right.

But the real power in the room belonged to Mrs. Wilson.

I sat at my desk, head down, barely breathing, trying to disappear as
her eyes swept the room, searching for her next target.
My stomach twisted. The bologna sandwich threatened a comeback.

Her gaze hovered like a spotlight—cold, calculating, waiting for weakness.
She didn't just command the room.
She cornered it.

Mrs. Wilson never raised her voice. She didn't have to.
It was the way she carried herself: sharp, deliberate, always watching.
The click of her heels carried the threat.

Squeak. Step. Squeak. Step.
She paced the aisles, orthopedic soles betraying her steely presence—
footsteps like a metronome, counting down to someone's inevitable
doom.

Squeak. Pause. Squeak.

I'd seen it a hundred times. The scan. The narrowed eyes. A predator
sizing up her prey.
She never picked the eager ones. She liked to watch people squirm.

The Wilson Freeze.
A spell you couldn't shake once her eyes found you.

One time, she picked Robbie—a quiet kid in the back.
He froze, mouth half-open, words gone. She waited. Tapped her
nails on her clipboard.
The silence stretched until the whole class held its breath.
Finally, she sighed and moved on.

But the damage was done. Robbie didn't speak for a week.

That's what she did. She tested you.

And I was *not* about to be the next Robbie.

I angled my shoulders—not too much, not too little.
Just enough to seem present, engaged, but not available.
Eye contact was the kiss of death.

I focused on the tiny dent on my desk, tracing its grooves with my
fingertip, willing myself to disappear.
Not me. Not this time.

✦

Then—second grade. The spelling bee.
I had studied for days, convinced I could win. Practiced holding the
trophy—the one on the bookshelf next to the fish tank.
My name was called. I stood at the front, heart pounding, socks
slipping in too-big sneakers.

The word was "umbrella." Easy, right? I knew it. *I knew I knew it.*

But my mind went blank. Just... gone.

Laughter. Whispers. One cough that shattered the silence.
Then the dreaded blare of the teacher's bell—sharp, merciless, final.

I sank into my seat and burned the rest of the day.
Couldn't look at anyone. Not even Cassie.

Being put on the spot wasn't an opportunity.
It was a trap I couldn't escape.

✦

Across the room, eager Tracy practically vibrated in her seat, hand shooting up with enough force to cause wind resistance.
Pick her. Pick her. PICK HER.

She was *that* girl.
The one who thrived on participation. Who lived for the teacher's approval.
Who probably practiced raising her hand in the mirror.
I, on the other hand, was *not* that girl.
I was shy. *Painfully shy.*
The kind of shy that twisted my stomach into knots at the thought of speaking out loud.
Where attention felt suffocating.
Where being in a crowded room felt like too much.

And yet, even then, I knew how to read a room.
I knew when to shrink. When to smile enough to slide by.

Survival wasn't about being invisible.
It was about being forgettable—*at least until it was safe to be seen.*

the selection

And then—the squeaking stopped. Right next to me.

I held my breath.
Mrs. Wilson's gaze landed on me.

No. No, no, no.

Not an invitation—a selection.
The kind chosen by queens. Or hunters.

The temperature dropped.
The kids stiffened, breath held.

She skipped right over Tracy—ignoring the desperate flailing—and in
that measured, icy voice:

"Taira, would you please stand up and share with the class what you
read this week?"

My whole body locked.
The room tilted.
A sharp pulse in my ears.
My face burned.

Shit.

I thought about running—making a break for the door.
But my body betrayed me, locking me in place.
Sweating. Dizzy.
I might pass out.

Across the room, my best friend Cassie caught my eye and gave me
a small, almost imperceptible nod.
You got this.

She was the only one who knew I practiced in the mirror.
Knew how much this moment terrified me.
Knew that last week, I made her sit on my bed while I read the whole
thing aloud—twice.
Made her promise not to laugh even if my voice cracked.

She was my safe place.
Even when everything else felt like a test.

I wasn't sure I *got this.*

But somehow, I forced my legs to move, pushed my chair back, and stood.
I gripped my notebook like a lifeline, holding it too high—like I could
shield myself from their stares.
Knees wobbling. Fingers white-knuckled.
I was sure everyone could see how hard I was trying to hold it together.

I *hated* this—how my voice always hid when I needed it most.
How my hands trembled.
Pulse pounding like a warning drum.

Mrs. Wilson waited. The class waited.
I swallowed.

And then—somehow—found my voice.

pippi and the pulse

"Once upon a time..."

I had worked on this for hours—reading, re-reading, rehearsing in my
room when no one was listening.
I knew the words.
That didn't make them easier to say.

Pippi Longstocking.
No parents. No rules. No one telling her what to do.

I read that book cover to cover—sitting on the floor, legs crisscrossed
by my bed, lamplight like a spotlight, while my sister blasted *Forever
Young* through the wall.
I wanted to believe I had even an ounce of that wildness in me.

But instead, I was standing in a classroom, gripping my notebook with
sweaty palms, praying I wouldn't faint.

Maybe I wasn't as fearless as I thought.
Maybe I envied how she didn't care what anyone thought.
Maybe I wanted to know what it felt like—to stomp around in
mismatched socks, with wild red braids, living in my own world,
untouched by judgment.

But that wasn't me.
Still, the words kept coming.
My voice steadied. Sentence by sentence, I stopped reading—and
started speaking.

I finished my report and braced for... *I don't know*—a polite nod? *Nothing?*

Instead—clapping.
Actual clapping.
A few cheers.

The sound hit me like a wave—loud, dizzying, almost too much.
My chest squeezed tight—I forgot how to breathe.
I finally exhaled—like I'd been holding tension in my ribs all week.

My shoulders dropped, my hands relaxed—and for the first time all
day, my feet felt planted.

Wait—did I actually do that?

My body thrummed, like I'd stepped into someone braver—and she
decided to stay.

I did it.

And the weight changed.
Not just relief. Something almost like hope.

Maybe I wasn't trapped in the shy version of me.
Maybe fear wasn't the whole story.
The Freeze didn't break me.

When I think back on that moment, it's not only the fear I remember.
It's the applause.
The rush.
The possibility.

I didn't know it then, but something loosened.
Opened.
Let light in.

Maybe Pippi wasn't so far away after all.
Maybe she'd been here the whole time—waiting for her cue.

＋

double life in leg warmers

Split life. Full volume.

split identities

At that age, my world was a mash-up of contradictions.
One minute, I was destined for leg warmers and a *Flashdance*-style
audition montage; the next, I was solving mysteries with the
Scooby-Doo gang.

Most kids picked a lane.
You were either the girl dancing to *What a Feeling* in the mirror—or the
one yelling,
It was the guy in the rubber mask!
Me? I refused to choose.

The living room was my stage. And my crime scene.
The hardwood floor doubled as a Broadway rehearsal space and a
hidden lair with invisible tripwires.
I'd leap across the room, twirling like Jennifer Beals—then drop to
the ground, carefully avoiding the "laser beams" guarding my
imaginary treasure.

The soundtrack? *Love Is a Battlefield.*
I didn't know the lyrics—but I felt them.
The tension. The drama.
I imagined I was fighting for freedom. For truth. Or the right to dance
however I wanted.

At some point, I even tried singing along.

Bad idea.

My voice cracked.

I couldn't find the melody—even if it had a spotlight and waved.

My best effort landed like a sad, off-key B-flat. *Bless its heart.*

A tribute—but not a good one.

One second, I was basking in a spotlight, waiting for my final bow.

The next, I was crouched behind the couch, notebook in hand,
documenting suspicious parental behavior.

Suspect One: Mom. Has been in the kitchen for over an hour.

Pretends not to see me.

Suspect Two: Dad. Whispered something to Mom.

Possible secret mission.

Case File: WHAT ARE THEY HIDING?

I once followed them around for an entire afternoon, convinced I'd
uncover a family secret.

All I saw was my dad shove something into the closet and tell me to go play.

I wrote it down anyway.

I took everything seriously. Dance. Mysteries. All of it.

Because Daphne didn't wait to be rescued—she was smart. Poised.

In control.

And Jennifer Beals didn't want to dance—she *had* to.

I didn't know which version of me was real yet.

But I liked that I didn't have to choose.

Maybe they didn't know how to handle my imagination.
So they did what most busy parents do: signed me up for everything
and hoped something stuck.

the first step

My parents had a business to run, which meant they didn't always
have time for me.
Their solution was simple: keep me busy.
If I wasn't at home, I couldn't get into trouble.
If I was always learning something, I was being productive.

Like getting dropped off at a babysitter—except instead of watching
cartoons, I was supposed to be gaining skills.
So I became a serial student.

Gymnastics, week after week—until one backflip made me rethink life.
Singing lessons—a complete disaster. Tone-deaf. Hopeless.
Piano felt like decoding hieroglyphics.
Ice skating? One fall and I was out.

Then the gymnastics studio shut down—and in its place, a dance
studio opened.
The windows were fogged with breath and motion.
The door smelled like hairspray and leather soles.
I peeked inside once and saw someone spinning, arms wide, like she
was flying.
Intense, but in a different way—less danger, more drama.
Honestly? Thank God.

So when my parents asked if I wanted to try dance, I shrugged.
Okay, sure. Why not?
It wasn't some epic moment of destiny. *No lightning bolt.*
It was another class.
Or so I thought.

The first thing I remember? The floor.
Not cold and hard like the ice rink.
Not springy like the gymnastics mat.
Smooth. Light. Almost soft—like it was made for movement.

The music filled the room—louder than I expected.
Not background noise.
Something you could feel.
It moved through you before your brain even caught up.

And the mirrors—so many.
Everywhere I turned, there I was—no hiding, no fading into the background.
Me.
Every awkward angle, every hesitant step, reflected a thousand times over.

My stomach tightened. I tried not to stare too long.

Then I saw Jamie from school.
We weren't close, but I admired her—confident, funny, sure of herself.
Definitely not new to this.

I, on the other hand, had no idea what I was doing.

"Follow along," she whispered.

And something in me let go.

At school, I was shy. Careful. Always trying to stay small, stay neutral,
stay unnoticed.

But with Jamie?

It didn't feel intimidating.

It felt... *possible.*

The music started, and I was behind.

The other girls moved like they'd been born knowing—perfect arms,
clean landings.

I was half a beat late, trying to fake it.

The instructor—graceful, grounded—glided across the floor.

"Again," she said, clapping to the beat.

My face burned. *Again?*

I glanced at Jamie. She wasn't flustered.

She moved like she belonged here.

Whereas I wasn't sure I did.

I became hyper-aware—

feet meeting floor, arms misfiring.

Tense here, floppy there.

Like my limbs were freelancing.

So I broke it down like a detective.

Where should my weight be?

Why did my right side move easier than my left?

Maybe I didn't know all the steps.
Maybe I wasn't polished.
But movement?
That, I understood.

I didn't need to be perfect—I needed to move.

Then something clicked.
I locked into the rhythm.
The pulse.
The part of me that knew.

For the first time, I wasn't copying.
I was feeling it.

When class ended, Jamie asked,
"Are you coming back next week?"

I didn't hesitate.
"Yeah, I think so."

julie rules

She owned the studio.
Not with volume—but with presence.
Elegant. Grounded. Magnetic.
She didn't need to intimidate.
Her stillness carried weight.
You straightened without realizing.

She didn't dance—she embodied it.
When she moved, something stirred in me—quiet but powerful.
I wanted her grace. Her quiet authority.
It felt like the room tuned itself to her frequency.

I looked up to her instantly.
And for whatever reason, she looked back.
Maybe it was my hunger—how I threw myself in, desperate to get it right.
Whatever it was, she saw me.
Worked with me.
Pushed me.
Believed in me.

One afternoon, I kept falling out of a turn. Wobbly. Off-balance.
Frustrated.
Julie watched, then stepped closer.
"You're using your arms," she said. "Your core—your center—is what
turns you. Without it, you'll never land it."

I tried again. It finally connected. A flicker of understanding.
Julie nodded.
"Good. Again."

A spark lit in my chest—small, fragile, but real.
Someone believed I could be *more than just okay.*
Her gift: pushing you to the edge, never letting you fall.

She became more than a teacher.
She was a compass.
She saw something in me I hadn't seen yet.
And for the first time, I started to see it too.

What started as a class became something else.
Not a hobby. Not an outlet.
An identity.

A few months in, we had a studio showcase.
Nothing fancy—scratchy tutus, folding chairs, camcorders in the back.
It wasn't Broadway—*but in my heart, it was.*

The music started—and I wasn't scared. *I was alive.*
Every count. Every step. Every smile—*clicked.*

That was the moment it all lit up.
My first recital sealed it.
I stepped onto that stage—and never wanted to step off.

Julie opened the door.
She didn't stay my teacher for long, but she stayed in my life.
And what she sparked in me never left.

hooked

At first, it was one class a week. Then two. Then three.
Before I knew it, I was there every other day.

I loved the way my body could move—twisting, turning, spinning.
I could take up space without apologizing for it.
Somehow, it all made sense.

I'd never been the type to sit still—and now, I didn't have to.
I could leap. Stretch. Spin in circles until I got dizzy—and no one
told me to stop.

Dance took over everything.
I walked like I was rehearsing.
Marked combinations in line at the store.
Stretched in the kitchen.
Practiced turns in the hallway.
At night, I replayed routines before sleep—body twitching with
moves I hadn't even mastered.

I started walking differently—shoulders back, posture straight—like I
was already standing at the barre.
I was moving—and fully aware.
Of space. Of my body. Of how everything connected.

And music?
It wasn't just background noise—it became my teacher.
I broke down songs, counted beats, imagined movement.
Could this be a turn sequence? Would this work for a leap?
Every song had its own pull.
A pattern. A possibility.

I wasn't just learning dance.
I was beginning to *see* it—everywhere.

And best of all—I wasn't alone.
Jamie and I had gotten closer.
Through her, I started talking to other girls in class.

It wasn't like school, where friendships felt like exclusive clubs you
had to fight your way into.
Here, it felt different.
More open.
More fun.
More... *me.*

We laughed when someone fell out of a turn.
Cheered when someone nailed a pirouette.
Gave each other tips.
Shared gum.
Tied each other's shoes.

Dance brought people together.
We didn't need matching personalities or perfect hair.
Only music—and space to move.

Maybe that's why I kept showing up.
It wasn't about the music or the movement alone.
It was about *belonging*.
And that was worth sticking around for.

At dance, I could finally breathe.
At school, I folded.
Tense.
Alert.
Scanning for threats.

Looking back, it was more than a double life.
Two versions of me—*one trying to disappear, the other learning to take up space.*
It was choreography.
Two roles. Two worlds.
And I was performing both—*trying not to drop the act.*

✦

mean girl mandate

Nothing says friendship like synchronized ignoring.

the hate committee

One day, I was existing.
The next? I was a target.

I could feel it—like a drop in air pressure.
That sudden, unspoken Mean Girl Council vote that I was now the enemy.
Like they'd flipped a switch.
Like they'd been waiting for an excuse.

A single, casual, passing *Hey*.
That's all it took.

Stacy's boyfriend said hi to me in the hallway.
Not a flirty *Hey*.
Not a *meet-me-behind-the-bleachers* kind of *Hey*.
Just a meaningless, half-hearted hallway *Hey*.
I didn't even say anything back—kept walking, trying not to get
flattened in the passing period rush.
But Stacy noticed. And that was enough.

It didn't matter that I wasn't interested.
That I barely made eye contact.
To them, it was betrayal.
To me, it was baffling.

Stacy had an entourage: four, sometimes five girls—a fully functioning middle school hate committee, self-appointed and fueled by insecurity.

They were a walking cliché: Aqua Net–infused '80s hair, misted into helmets for their fragile egos; oversized sweatshirts with the collars cut off (*Flashdance had us all in a chokehold*); scrunched socks over high-top Reeboks; hoop earrings that jingled with every hair flip; and layers of Bonne Bell lip gloss, weaponized under fluorescent lights.

The boldest wore a swipe of blue eyeliner that said,
Yeah. I wear makeup now.

Every outfit was calculated. Matching. Strategic.
They weren't just a group. They were a brand.
And God forbid one of them stepped out of sync.

They moved as a pack.
Standing alone was too risky.
They were rehearsed—dancers in a performance of dominance.

What they didn't realize was that I was a dancer too.
Playing a different role.

At the top of their pyramid of pettiness was Stacy.
Ringleader. Puppet master. Queen of fake.
If she was mad, they were mad.
She whispered like a teen movie villain. They nodded on cue.
One opinion. One brain cell. Passed around like shared lip gloss.

At first, the bullying was small.
A locker slammed in my face.

Whispers loud enough to overhear.
A spitball landing in my hair during class.

Annoying? Yes.
Scary? Not yet.
But it wore on me—the constant murmuring, the sideways glances,
the sudden quiet when I entered a room.

Even when they weren't saying anything, they said everything.

Not monsters. Not even brave.
Bored girls with bad instincts, chipping at what they didn't understand: *me.*
I didn't orbit their approval or play their games.
I had my own rhythm. My own world.
And that scared them.

Everywhere I turned, they were there.
At lockers. In the cafeteria.
Snickering over juice boxes and nachos.

Even the boyfriend who'd innocently greeted me told Stacy to leave
me alone—which only made things worse.
They saw it as proof.
Me recruiting him. Stealing their crown.
Infiltrating their cardboard kingdom.

Eventually, it wasn't even about me.
It was about control. Rank. Keeping the performance running.

I hadn't meant to disrupt their script.
But sometimes, even the tiniest crack breaks the whole scene.

They weren't terrifying. They were relentless.
Mosquitoes buzzing, carrying an emotional virus.

And I was starting to feel infected.

I showed up every day feeling a little less like myself.
It's strange—how you can feel so *watched*, so *scrutinized*—
and yet *completely invisible.*

Didn't cry. Didn't flinch.
Didn't tell anyone.
But it got in.

It showed in my posture—shoulders caving, books clutched like a
shield, eyes scanning hallways before stepping out.
Death by a thousand whispers.
But under pressure, something always has to give.
Not here. Not in the studio.

in the studio, nothing changed

At school, I was shrinking.
At dance, I was sweating.
Julie demanded perfection.
"Your shoulders—drop them."
"Again."
"Breathe."

She didn't care if I'd had a bad day.
Didn't care that I was unraveling.
Didn't ask. She kept pushing.

And somehow, I loved her for that.
Hated her too, sometimes.
But mostly loved her.

In a world that felt like it was slipping out from under me, Julie was
gravity.

I remember one night—after fighting with my parents and enduring
another hallway ambush of whispers and glances—I showed up to
class on the verge of tears.
Barely holding it together. Jaw tight. Neck stiff. Breath shallow.

We couldn't work it out—me and my parents.
No matter how hard I tried, they didn't hear me.

But Julie didn't need the full story.
She never asked what was wrong.
She looked at me. *Really* looked.

Mid-combo, she walked by and lifted my elbow gently into place—
a tiny correction, like resetting a compass.
Not a word. Not a pause. Then moved on.

She didn't care that my voice was stuck in my throat.
She needed my form to be right.
Didn't coddle. Didn't console.

But in her calm—something solid. Something grounding.
Like she was saying: *I see you. But you're still capable.*

Her expectations were high. And they didn't waver.
She didn't need to save me. She needed to not flinch.

That was the difference.
Everyone else either looked away—
or looked too closely.
Julie held steady.

I was holding back tears in the mirror, trying to keep count, trying
not to fall behind.
Julie clapped her hands: "Start from the top."
No mercy.

Dance helped me breathe again.
The studio was the only place my body didn't feel foreign.
Julie gave me something to focus on—something to fight for.

Something to believe in.
Even if it was a clean pirouette.

Here there were no excuses. No room for weakness.
No vanishing act.

And in some strange way, that was exactly what I needed.

Because when the rest of the world was picking me apart in whispers,
I needed one place—*one*—where I could fight to stay whole.

Even when I was falling apart inside, I showed up.
Even when the mean girls had sucked all the air out of my day, I came
to class.
Even when I was exhausted from faking it, I danced.

The studio didn't ask me to explain.
It asked me to keep showing up.
And I did.

The mirrors didn't talk back.
The choreography didn't change.
The rules made sense.

Not perfect.
Didn't fix everything.
But it gave me ground to stand on.

my voice, my church

I didn't have the language for it then.
I knew school was war.
And dance was *air.*

Every insult made me want to disappear—
but the studio gave me another option.
I could vanish into movement.
Or better: I could *speak* through it.

Dance was mine.
No one could touch it.
Not the girls whispering behind my back.
Not the boys who laughed because they didn't get it—
and *never would.*
Not even the things we never talked about at home.

It belonged to me.
And I got to decide what it meant.

It was sacred.
Like church is for some people.
A place to lay it all down—the noise, the shame, the hurt.
I left it on the floor and came out lighter.

It became my voice when I didn't have one.
My freedom when everything else felt like a cage.

I held onto it because it mattered.
Because it reminded me who I was.
Because it whispered—*you still have power.*

And now?
Now I see it even more clearly.
The joy. The people. The spark of it all.
What a gift.

I wouldn't change any of it.
Not even the mean girls.

Back then, it cut deep.
I thought it meant something about me.

But now I know better.
It wasn't about me.
It was about them.

A projection—
not a reflection.

who would even believe me?

Back then, I didn't have a name for it.
I just thought it was *me.*

It was quiet, but not safe.
Like being watched and ignored at the same time.
A kind of isolation that didn't make a sound—
but somehow echoed.

No slurs. No bruises.
Just slights, stacked until something cracked.

Tension.
Eye rolls.
Laughter that paused when I walked by.
A whisper meant to be heard.
A note in my backpack: *Ugh.*

Are they actually doing something? Or am I being sensitive?

That was the genius of it—
they made you question your sanity while they sharpened the blade.

So I told no one.
Not my parents. Not my teachers. Not even Jamie.

But she knew.

I kept dancing. Kept pretending I was fine.
But Jamie saw past the performance.

"What's going on?" she asked one night after class, stretching beside
me on the studio floor.

"Nothing."
Eyes down. Thread pulled loose. A knot in my throat.

"They're not worth it," she said—casual, certain.
Like she already knew.
Maybe not the story, but the weight.

I hadn't told anyone.
But even that small crack in the silence let air in.
"Yeah, I know," I muttered.

That was all. She didn't push.
But her words stayed.

Because part of me needed to believe it—
that I was bigger than their petty nonsense.
That one day, their names wouldn't matter.

I wasn't there yet.
Still walking the same halls.
Still trying to stay upright.

The longer it went, the louder it got.
Whispers sharpened.
Stares lingered.
It felt like they were waiting to watch me break.

By then, it wasn't teasing.
It was erosion.
A slow wear.

I told myself I could outlast them.
But the truth?

I was tired.
So *tired.*

One day, after yet another whisper I wasn't supposed to hear, I thought:

How much more of this are you willing to take?
How long will you swallow it just to keep the peace?

No one was coming.
And silence was its own surrender.

So I made a choice:
I wasn't carrying it alone anymore.

.

the underdogs & the mission

I always thought I was superhuman—like *Pippi Longstocking*.
Like I was meant to protect.
But before I could do that, I had to learn to stand up for myself.

That realization hit back in elementary school.

We were by the tetherball.
Recess chaos all around—screaming kids, jump ropes whipping,
basketballs crashing into chain nets.
Some boy said something to me—I don't even remember what.
A joke, a jab, something designed to embarrass me.

Chest tight.
Cheeks flushed.
I wanted to disappear.

But before I could think, my foot moved without permission.
I kicked him.
Right in the balls.

One second he was laughing.
The next, he was gasping like a fish out of water.

The whole playground went still.
And for the first time ever, I wasn't prey.

I was powerful.

Then came the shame.
I didn't want to be *that* girl.
Didn't want to turn mean.
But I also didn't want to be small.
I wanted to know I mattered.

I hadn't meant to hurt him.
I reacted—like my body made the decision before my brain could catch up.
And that's when it hit me:
Standing up for myself wasn't the problem.
I needed better timing. Sharper aim.

That instinct—to push back, to protect—never really left.
It lived in me like a low hum.
A warning system.
A siren song.

I always rooted for the underdogs.
The weird kids. The loners.
The ones who ate lunch alone or got picked last for dodgeball.
Didn't matter what color team you were on—if you were getting
picked on, I had to step in.

It was a secret mission from the universe.
A silent rule etched in my bones:

If I didn't step in, I'd feel it later.
In my gut. In my chest.
In the part of me that couldn't stand to watch it happen.

Something flipped that day.
The part that stayed quiet.
That let things slide.
That tried to keep the peace, even when it hurt—
gave way to something else.

The part that was ready to fight.
To speak up.
To reclaim her space.

Turns out, coiled thunder makes a damn great fuse.
They picked the wrong girl to underestimate.
The fire was already lit.
The choice was already forming.

I could keep playing small.
Or I could finally take up space.
Even if it scared me.
Even if I stood alone.

I didn't know how it would play out.
But I knew one thing for sure:

I wasn't going to shrink.
And I wasn't going to become the kind of girl who dimmed others to
feel brighter.

A win without the mean-girl makeover.

✦

combat & cafeteria politics

You don't have to swing to win.

prepared to punch, too soft to swing

This part makes me cringe—but it's the truth.

Before I made my bold move to call them out, I had a friend, Dara.
She was older. Wiser.
She'd had enough of the bullying too.

One day, she pulled me aside, locked eyes, and said:
"Get your shit together. Fight back."

Not the advice I expected.
But I trusted her.

So—Fight Camp was born.
And yes, it was *dead* serious.

• Hair slicked back tight (to prevent hair pulling, obviously)
• Braces slathered in wax
• Knee-high socks under my jeans
• Vaseline on my face—because apparently, it made punches slide off
• No mouthguard—but plenty of pep talks from a girl who'd never been
in a fight either

Okay, let's pause.
What was I thinking?
Who. Did. I. Think. I. Was?!

Training for an underground cafeteria brawl—
or trying not to cry in the lunch line?

Fight Club: 8th Grade Edition.
And we trained.

Shadowbox. Drill fake punches. Practice being mad. (*Not my strong suit.*)

Pretending to be mad felt about as natural as dissecting a frog in
chem—
all smell, nausea, and silent dread.
And those poor butterflies—we were supposed to pin them down,
pull them apart.
All I ever wanted to do was set them free.

And now? *I was greased up for combat.*

They say it takes strength to admit your weaknesses.
If that's true, maybe *I was stronger than I thought.*

Once, I landed on my ass—mid-fake punch—and totally forgot I was
supposed to be angry.
We burst out laughing—ugly, full-body laughter—the kind that makes
you forget why you were mad to begin with.

Then she'd reset, wipe the smile off, and go, "Again."

We ran scenarios:
What if she grabs your arm?
What if they all charge at you?

She even taught me how to take a hit—just in case.

And yep—we kept it going. For weeks.

Looking back now, maybe it wasn't only about me.
Her home life was rough. Her dad was mean. Controlling.
The kind of man who let his frustrations spill over—hardest on the
people closest to him.

Maybe Dara was training me
to be the fighter
she couldn't be.

something finally broke in me

Then came the final straw.

I was at my locker. Out of the corner of my eye, I saw them—moving
in formation, like synchronized sharks.
I don't remember what I was wearing. I remember pretending to dig
for something, anything. Bracing like a soldier before impact.

Palms sweating.
Legs numb.
Throat tight.

Slo-mo: a hand shot out—fast, sharp—and grabbed my locker.
SLAM.

They tried to shut it on me.
But without thinking, I caught it mid-close.

That was it—no going back.

At some point, the training stopped feeling ridiculous.
No more second-guessing.
Maybe I wasn't a fighter—
but I wasn't prey anymore.

Once fear gave way to instinct, I didn't hesitate.

I didn't yell.
I looked her in the eye.
"Outside. Now."

The hallway froze.

Stacy's smirk twitched—barely.
One of her girls shifted beside her.
Someone exhaled through their nose.
No one said a word.

My heart slammed against my ribs.
But I didn't move.

And in that razor-thin moment between pause and reaction, the questions hit:
Was I really about to throw down?
Was I seriously ready to throw hands in the middle of the school hallway?
What if she'd said yes?

I didn't know.
Didn't care.
All I had was adrenaline—and a line they weren't crossing.

Then—finally—Stacy scoffed. Rolled her eyes.
"She's crazy," one of them muttered.

But they backed off.

I stood frozen—still bracing for something that never came.
Then the tremors—tiny, invisible tremors, like my muscles had been
holding their breath.

I exhaled.
Finally.

Not brave.
Not proud.
Just... relieved.
Exhausted.
Inside out.

Was that really me?

I didn't recognize myself.
Maybe that was the point.

I was done.
And to be honest, I was as shocked as they were.

Was I really going to fight them all? Roundhouse kick someone in the hallway?
No clue—I hadn't thought that far ahead.

Turns out—I didn't have to.

Because just like that—boom.
I expected a scoff. A shove. Some kind of retaliation...

But instead...
Static.
Stares.
A hesitation I'd never seen before.
A nervous chuckle.
A step back.

And then—it turned.

They all backed down.
The bullying stopped.
I was no longer their target.

One week ago, they were launching spitballs at me.
Now they were linking arms—smiling like we'd been best friends all along.

Was this a sick joke—or was I supposed to say thank you?

They invited me to their lunch table—like this had all been some
kind of test I'd passed.
Like I'd *earned* my place.
And I had no idea what to do with that.

It didn't feel like a win.
It felt... suspicious.
Maybe a softer form of control.

I wasn't sure I liked it.
But I played along. For a little while.

Did life get easier?
In some ways, yeah.

But I couldn't shake the feeling that the only reason they "respected"
me now...
was because I *forced* them to.

And honestly?
That felt as fake as their friendship.

So, after a while, I drifted away.
I had bigger things to focus on.

I didn't land a punch.
But I rewrote the rules.

And after that—
they kept their distance.

No swing.
No scream.
Not a single nail lost.
I redrew the whole dynamic—
and walked away holding the pen.

That?
That was the real flex.

✦

karma keeps receipts

"Karma never loses an address." — Unknown

balance, restored

Mean people suck.
Seriously—how do you wake up every day and *choose* cruelty?
Don't you know about karma?
Well... good luck with that.

Karma scared me straight.
Probably why I always tried to do the right thing—because deep
down, I believed it: *what you put out comes back.*

I wasn't raised religious.
My parents were part-time Buddhist at best.
God wasn't part of the equation.
But karma? *That* made sense.

It was clean.
It was earned.

Do good, get good.
Do harm? *Brace yourself.*

That's why I always stepped in.
Even when it wasn't my fight.
Even when looking away was safer.

Because if karma was real—and I was betting it was—
I wanted to be on the right side of it.
Not perfect. Just not complicit.

And sometimes? Karma showed up right on schedule.

Like the day a new girl introduced herself during a group project—
voice trembling, vowels thick with *home*.
The others exchanged smirks.
She was doing her best.
But some people only see difference as weakness.

I remembered how small it made me feel—getting laughed at
for the way *I* spoke.
That's why I noticed.
And that's why I didn't feel bad when the universe returned the serve.

A few weeks later, one of those girls wiped out during a pep rally—
mid-cartwheel, center court, full-split fall in front of the entire school.
Cheer skirt up. Face beet red. Gym howling.

I didn't laugh—*out loud.*
But in my head: *Balance, restored.*

Or the time I bought my best friend a jacket.
A good one. Thoughtful. From the heart.
His girlfriend didn't like that.
Cruella de Stitch unpicked it—stitch by stitch—like a petty little
villain in a straight-to-VHS movie.
There was drama, a stomp, a kick—and yep, she broke her own foot.
Karma's got a flair for irony.

And then—years later—a guy I once dated circled back.
Back then, he acted like he was doing me a favor.
Same wink, same empty promise.
Still mistaking smug for substance.

He smiled and said,
"You're really doing well for yourself. Never would've guessed."

Like it was a compliment.
Like I should thank him for underestimating me.

I didn't flinch.
Didn't correct him.
I smiled back—because wow, that was the karma.

Karma doesn't always crash in.
Sometimes it simply lets them hear themselves out loud.

Turns out, you don't need to keep score when the universe already is.

✦

lost in translation—and then some

My accent disappeared.
Then I lost myself.

shapeshifter survival

A little background—
my parents did well for themselves. Immigrants who left everything
behind to start over in the U.S.

Life in Thailand was comfortable. A house. A German Shepherd. My
dad's furniture business, built from scratch.

My mom was the glue. Steady, practical, the one who held it together
when things got uncertain.
When the idea of America came up—bigger houses, better jobs, a
future where their daughters could become anything—they said yes.
Packed up and started over.

No safety nets. No guarantees. Just a dream—and each other.

We landed in a small desert town in Nevada.
Not quite L.A.—more like dry heat, dollar stores, and the occasional
jackrabbit.

I was five. My sister was seven.
And it was a culture shock.

You don't land in a new country and adjust overnight.
You feel everything unravel—routine, language, even your sense of self.

There's a stretch between who you were and who the world expects
you to become.

We were one of the only Asian families in town.
English wasn't my first language.
Even after I learned it, my accent made me feel like an outsider.

I got used to being misunderstood.
To hearing my name repeated like a riddle.
To kids mocking my parents' accents.

Too American at home—
too foreign everywhere else.

The hardest part wasn't the teasing.
It was the in-between—
that *not-this, not-that* feeling that followed me everywhere.

So I adapted.

Translated my parents' words.
Balanced their customs with cafeteria culture.
Smiled. Stayed polite.
At home, I honored the sacrifice.
At school, I tried to disappear.

I wanted to make them proud—
but I also wanted to trade snacks and eat pizza
without my thermos announcing itself with garlic and soy sauce.

Everyone else had Twinkies and cheese puffs.
I had a full-blown stir-fry situation.

I didn't want to be the same.
That came later, when I hated wearing the same outfit as anyone else.
I just didn't want to feel like an alien.

Assimilation wasn't a choice.
It was survival.

So I became a shapeshifter.
Code-switching before I even knew the term.
Laughing at jokes, even when they stung.
Thanking people instead of correcting them.

That kind of adapting takes a toll.
You start to wonder who you really are when no one's watching—
and which parts you buried to belong.

No one asked me to change.
But I did.
And for a long time,
I thought that meant I was doing it right.

the weight of hope

"This is where the blueprint began—
for watching, decoding, becoming.
For finding footing in a world that didn't speak my language."

Kindergarten was full-blown sensory overload.
The walls yawned. Voices came in waves.
Everything blurred—kids, teachers, rules I couldn't parse.

Even the crayons felt American—fat, waxy, cartoon-colored.
They didn't glide. They *shouted.*

We sat in a circle. One by one, each kid said their name and favorite food.
I panicked.
Not because I didn't know my name—but because I didn't know
what food to say.
My favorite was my mom's *kao tom*—a warm broth, rice, minced pork—
but I wasn't sure it had an English name.
So I blurted, "banana." *I hated bananas.* But it made everyone smile.

Later came snack time: graham crackers.
Everyone else tore into them like it was the highlight of the day.
I held mine like a math problem.
No frosting. No wrapper. Brown rectangles. Dry. Confusing.
A betrayal in snack form.

I didn't want to look weird—so I took a bite.
It turned to paste. Bland, dusty paste.
These kids were thrilled with cardboard.
Meanwhile, my taste buds were in mourning.

Then: "Why is your hair so shiny?"
I froze.
It didn't sound like a compliment—more like a question wrapped in judgment.
Crumbs stuck to my lips.
The look on my face said the rest.
He moved on, bored.
I stayed stuck—every layer of *other* stitched to my skin.

The room moved on, too—like they all knew the script.
Me? I wasn't even sure I was in the right story.

A lump formed in my throat. My stomach knotted.
I clenched my fists.
And in that swirl of nerves and not belonging...
I wet my pants. Right there, in the middle of the classroom.

That's how my American life began.
Not with a grand adventure.
Not with a hero's welcome.
Just a puddle of fear.

I didn't lose myself in translation.
I was becoming.
Learning words. Learning humor. Learning resilience.
One banana-lie, one graham-cracker bite, one shiny-haired breath at a time.

the language that betrayed us

At five, language isn't only words.
It's belonging.

I watched the other kids joke and shout across the playground—
words pouring out of them like water. Effortless.

I stayed quiet.
Not for lack of thought, but for lack of words.

So I nodded. Laughed when they laughed.
Mimicking became my survival tactic.

When you don't have the language, you read everything—tone,
gesture, timing.
A full-body guessing game.

I listened. Gathered fragments. Echoed TV shows. Rehearsed responses.
English sat in my mouth like a foreign object—clunky, unsure, never
mine.

By first grade, I was fluent.
By second, I could barely remember not knowing it.
By third, I was correcting my parents.

For them, Rs and Ls? Total minefield.
Th? A myth.
Vs? Practically didn't exist.

Rice became *lice*. Three became *tree*.
Very became *wery*—like a cartoon villain had rigged their script.

I'd mastered the language.
English had other plans for them.

I didn't make it easier.
Don't talk to me in Thai, I'd mutter—
as if shame could help me blend in.

And then—the guilt hit.
Was I protecting my English?
Or just embarrassed?
Probably both.

At school, I walked a tightrope.
Hearing my parents call my name in Thai made me wince.
So I cut them off—answered in English, pretended not to hear, rushed
the conversation along.

With every new word, an old one disappeared.
I missed Thai's soft vowels—
the way my mom's voice sounded like home.
Even soup felt foreign—like a language we no longer shared.

I didn't hate being Thai.
I just didn't know where it lived in me.

Language betrays you—then becomes you.
The words that once marked me as an outsider—they're mine now.
But at what cost?

I thought fluency meant I belonged.
Instead, I learned how to bury what made me different.

luxury and lessons

My parents chased the best.
If it didn't cost enough, it wasn't good enough.

So when I brought home drugstore makeup—Wet n Wild, maybe CoverGirl—
I thought I'd struck gold.

To my dad? *Blasphemy.*
He marched me back to the store like I'd committed grand theft beauty.
Made me hand it over like contraband—then drove me straight to Macy's.

Back then Macy's wasn't just a store.
It was status. A temple. A classroom.
And in the '80s, Lancôme was gospel.

Lancôme ranked alongside Estée Lauder, Costco vitamins, designer bags—
and those legendary muffins:
shrink-wrapped tighter than Yeezys on drop day,
massive berries bursting like confetti,
stuffed into carry-ons—pastries of prestige.

He didn't just buy a lipstick—he bought the whole counter:
skincare, toner, powder, the full Lancôme starter kit.

At first, I felt elevated—
the texture, the ritual, the glow.
Maybe he was right.

Then came the allergic twist:
my skin turned to sandpaper,
my lips swelled with regret.
The thing meant to elevate me rejected me.

All that status, all that pride—
gone in a puff of irritation and Benadryl.

That's when it hit me:
This wasn't about luxury—
it was *performance*—
and *performance* has a *price*.

my first foray into nails (and my first meltdown)

Some kids played with crayons.
I played with clear polish.

Harmless, right? Just a little gleam.

I sat on the floor, carefully painting each nail—tiny strokes of rebellion.
Grown-up, I thought.

Then—horror—my parents saw it.
Tore into me like I'd tattooed my knuckles.

It's clear! I wanted to scream.
But I just nodded like a criminal caught red-handed.
Took the lecture.
Absorbed the disappointment.
Filed it under *don't get caught*.

They didn't have to call me bad.
Their faces said enough: *slippery slope*.

First polish.
Next? A tube top on a party bus to hell.

A few days later, the polish started peeling.
Tiny slivers curling up at the edges.
Jagged strips flaking off.
Oh. My. God.

My nails were falling off—my actual nails.
Chest tight. Breath shallow. Full-body meltdown.

I sobbed like I was being disassembled.
Ran to my mom—hands trembling, tears, snot, and regret.

She blinked. Sighed.
Peeled it off in two seconds. Tossed it.

No lasting damage—just a seven-year-old in crisis over clear polish.

Lesson learned?
Maybe.
Clear polish today, chaos tomorrow.

final thought: finding myself in the in-between

I didn't grow up with one defined identity.
I grew up in translation—between languages, cultures, and the dreams my parents held versus the self I was still figuring out.

It wasn't just about words.
It was tone.
Context.
Subtext.

It wasn't always graceful.
Blisters from too-tight shoes.
Meltdowns over clear polish.

But beneath it was a blueprint.

Every stuttered sentence, every moment of shame, every Costco muffin smuggled through customs...
it added up.

At first: confusion.
Self-editing.
Hiding.

But it was building something—*quiet power.*
Soft armor.

I used to think the goal was to pick a side—
American enough. Thai enough. Something enough.

But the power wasn't in choosing.
It was in the *blend.*

In reading nuance like a native tongue.
In seeing from both the inside and outside.
In knowing your worth—*especially* when no one else does.

Belonging to yourself first.

I didn't just survive assimilation.
I turned it into something of my own.

And years later, piece by piece—
I found the parts I'd buried.
And invited them home.

✦

same same but different

Two sisters, two worlds.

outside the box

I didn't fit—at school or in the dance world.
So I leaned into the difference.

At home and in the studio, I was loud—expressive, even dramatic.
At school? Survival. Quiet. Careful.
A version of me built to blend.

Outside the box didn't feel lonely—*it felt like home.*

Maybe that's the hidden gift of being an immigrant kid:
You start life straddling two worlds, so you get comfortable in the in-between.
You watch, adapt, translate—picking up what others don't even know they're saying.

I used to think that made me lesser.
Now I know—it made me *layered.*

My parents didn't always understand dance, acting, fashion.
That's not what they'd crossed an ocean for.
But they gave me a life they couldn't imagine.
And I chose a path they couldn't imagine either.

There was guilt, at first.
But now? Gratitude.

I wasn't meant to follow.

I was meant to make my own lane.

I still remember the way certain Thai phrases landed in my ears:
"Be good." "Don't be dramatic." "Keep your head down."
Not cruelty—just protection, wrapped in parenting.

In the end, I wasn't built to dim.
And I was never that great at blending—no matter how hard I tried.

It felt like outsider energy was baked in from the start—
not just cultural, but something deeper.
Because even at home, with my sister,
it felt like we were speaking different tongues.

love, translated

We shared a room and a last name.
Not much else.

She was calm, quiet, practical.
I was fiery, emotional, slow to filter.
She made the honor roll. I made messes.
She smiled and stayed silent. I always asked why.

Team sports—volleyball, basketball, softball.
Built-in squad.
Weekend tournaments.
No time for lipstick.

Me? Sequins. Jazz hands. Invisible backup dancers.
Calluses on my feet. Late nights in the studio.
Still sketching my own map.

Her drawers were neat. Mine were war zones.
She liked order. I liked flair.
It drove her nuts.

We didn't play Barbies or dress-up together.
But Saturday mornings were sacred.
Smurfs. Scooby-Doo. Super Friends.
Two kids in footie pajamas—

lost in a cartoon-colored world.
Not trying to be different. *Only being.*

Then that one night: *Psycho II.*
Too young. Too unsupervised.
Clutching each other under the blanket during commercial breaks—
pretending we weren't scared.
We never talked about it again.
But for once, we were close.

She wasn't pretending. She wasn't performing.
She was steady. Present.

Meanwhile, I was a lot.
Bad hair days. Slammed doors. Broadway in the hallway.
She called it drama. I called it truth.

Looking back, I probably seemed ridiculous.
At the time, it was life or death.

She watched. Waited. Stayed still.
I jumped without looking.
No net. Pure instinct.

Some overreactions were quiet—
like pressing my lips smaller in the mirror,
trying to erase the parts that stood out.
Spoiler: didn't work.

We didn't fight, but we didn't bond either.
Satellites in the same sky.

Not because we didn't care—because we didn't know how.

She'd disappear into silence.
And I knew: interrupting wasn't the language of the house.
Keep moving. Keep quiet. Keep it in.
Emotions were clutter—tucked away before guests arrived.

We weren't raised with emotional vocabulary.
We were raised with endurance.

So we spoke in other ways.
Microwave notes. Silent rides.
Glances that said *I noticed.*

Same roof. Same orbit.
Still—something there.
A quiet kind of knowing.

Like when she'd wait outside the office if I got in trouble.
Or I'd come home to a Post-it after a hard day:
"Leftovers in the microwave."

She never said *I love you.*
But that note said it louder than anything else could.

It didn't look like hugs.
It looked like waiting.
Noticing.
Being there—without needing to explain why.

Same house. Same storm.
But we handled the weather differently.

She followed the map.
I scribbled mine in the margins.
Crumpled. Sharpie-marked. Still intact.

She never got in trouble.
I was the "Why can't you be more like your sister?" wildcard.
She got the gold star—while I melted down, blew up, held it in, and
let it all out.

But she wasn't faking it.
She was good.
Steady. Clear.

Her silence wasn't weakness.
My noise wasn't failure.
We were wired differently.

She showed me how to stay grounded.
I reminded her it was okay to take up space.

We weren't the whisper-secrets, talk-about-crushes sisters.
But we were teaching each other the whole time.

Still—
we made it home.

✦

sparkle, silence & survival

Spoiled in sequins. Forged in fire.
Glitter didn't save me. Grit did.

ava's studio, ava's rules

The studio? That was Ava's world.
A Japanese woman—barely five feet tall.
Tough as nails, stick-straight ponytail, the kindest smile you'd ever see.
She loved that place—you could feel it.
She ran it firm, focused, full of heart.
She took pride in it. And so did we.

We did competitions all over Northern California, two or three times a year.
Ava packed us into her Subaru—rain, snow, or shine.
Music on. Snacks packed. Costumes hanging in the back.

We took it seriously: matching jackets, hair slicked back, car rides full of whispered counts and nervous giggles.

We didn't win every time, but the trophies stacked up—
time capsules of effort and joy.

Ava didn't make a fuss.
A nod. A soft clap. A quiet "Good job today."
But her eyes said it all—she was proud.
She had built something. So had we.

And then there was Marty.
Marty didn't teach dance. He performed it.

He'd sashay in with fringe bouncing, short shorts daring you to say something.
Somehow, the bowtie made sense in that room.
A popped hip was his resting position.

He clapped between counts—loud, proud, dramatic applause, mostly for himself.
He deserved it.
Legs for days. Confidence that entered the room before he did.
Gay. Fabulous. Unmissable. *Always on.*

I stood right behind him and mimicked everything.
One ripple behind his ripple—trying to catch his fire, like maybe it could spread.

I watched with wide eyes as he danced like no one had ever told him to dim it.
Like the stage was wherever he stood.
Like softness didn't belong on the floor.

Watching Marty wasn't just choreography—
It was church.
Theater.
Rebellion.
Freedom.
All rolled into one sweat-drenched routine.

He showed me how to be loud in my body.
How to take up space.
How to perform the hell out of life—even when no one's clapping.

how they showed love

One night at the studio, I was frustrated as hell.
I couldn't hit this move—tried it over and over.
It simply wouldn't click.

My mom sat behind the viewing window—waiting.
Patient. Never rushed me.
But I cracked. Tears. Frustration.
All I wanted was to get it right.
That perfectionist streak was already setting in.

She didn't cheer. Or coach. Or critique.
She watched—her way of saying, *I see you.*

Asian parents from their generation didn't always express their emotions.
Not with hugs. Not with *I love you.*

But they showed up.
They stayed.
And for a kid who wanted to be seen—that was everything.

My dad showed love his own way.
Not with long talks or hugs—but with actions.
He'd slip me cash in secret when my mom wasn't looking—
a quiet handshake of affection—unspoken, but understood.

It was code:
You're special.
You're mine.
You're taken care of.

I was spoiled.
Absolutely a daddy's girl.

They made sure I never went without—
and accidentally created a monster.

A tantrum-throwing, sparkle-obsessed little monster.
Not evil. Utterly extra.
Codependent with limited-edition lip gloss.

I wasn't born materialistic.
I learned early: love came with receipts.

loud and quiet survival

If I wanted something, I didn't ask—I demanded.
And if I didn't get it? Instant meltdown. Floor. Screaming.
No buildup. No negotiation.

Looking back? *Pretty sad.*
But I didn't know any other way. Neither did they.

I love you rarely left their lips.
I, on the other hand, said it all the time—no response.
Just... *more presents.*

It took years to train them to say the words.
Years of repeating *I love you* until they finally, awkwardly, muttered
it back.
The first time they did, I nearly fainted.

So when words failed me, I filled the silence—with volume.
The tantrums stopped. But the mindset stuck.
I turned it inward.

Perfection wasn't about impressing anyone.
It was about control.

If I got it right, maybe the world would make sense.
If they said no, I found another way.

If something fell short, I kept searching.
If life didn't hand it to me, I built it myself.
It wasn't about being spoiled—
it was about certainty. A refusal to settle.

I didn't think I had that much.
Turns out, my normal wasn't universal.

In our house, love didn't come in words.
It came in crisp bills, folded tight and slipped under the table.
Conflict wasn't resolved—it was ignored until it hardened into silence.

Settling wasn't an option.
It was something other people did.

I didn't realize how different that was—
until I stepped outside of it.

And then there was my sister. *The saint.*
The one who never rocked the boat or asked for much.

I kicked and screamed. She kept the peace.

I was the loud one. The indulged one.
The one they weren't quite sure how to contain.

I'm sure she had her own ways of coping—quiet rebellions,
unspoken grief.
But I was too consumed with my world to notice.
At least, not back then.

Now? I see it more clearly.

We both lived in a house where love was real—rarely spoken.

And we each translated it in our own way: *me, loudly. Her, quietly.*

We didn't walk the same path.

Didn't even pack the same gear.

But we survived the same house—together.

Somewhere in the middle—between glitter and quiet—

we learned to listen for each other.

✦

family ties (or lack thereof)

Not "I love you." Just: "Did you eat?"

split branches

I wasn't close to most of my extended family.
Family on paper—but roots don't mean much when no one speaks.

Years ago, I did 23andMe and ended up staring at sixty pages of
connections—over 1,500 relatives.
A digital family tree—absurdly leafy.
But no one was climbing it.

None of them reached out. Neither did I.
If the closer ones weren't calling, this batch didn't stand a chance.
Granted—half of them were like... tenth cousins.

The trait results were hilarious.
Apparently, I have "50/50 chance of fearing public speaking," I'm "more
prone to stretch marks," and "likely to have a unibrow."
23andMe basically called me shaky, textured, and slightly furry.
Also—"likely to wake up around 7:21 a.m."
Weirdly specific. Disturbingly accurate.

We didn't do the big, American-style family reunions you see in movies.
No potato salad. No matching T-shirts.
No cousins screaming over slip-and-slides while grandmas piled
seconds on your plate.

Instead, we had silences.
Grudges that aged like wine—but soured like milk.
Stories passed down more through tension than tradition.

Some of it was petty.
Some of it was legit.
Most of it was so old, no one remembered how it started—or that it did.

Like my mom's older sister—the one married to the chopstick factory guy.
Fancy house. Private tennis club. Constant air of superiority.
The rest of the family didn't like her.
She didn't care.

Then there was my cousin in Thailand.
One visit, she pulled me aside like we were in a spy movie.
"Help us get out," she said.
Eyes darting. Breath shaky.

She and her boyfriend wanted to start over in the States, but the family didn't approve of him—which made it messier.
I was a teenager. What was I supposed to do about an international escape plan?

And my uncle—the one who lost his job and vanished to a ten-day silent retreat.
He came back lighter. Brighter.
Like he'd finally put his ghosts down.
I don't know what he found in that stillness, but I admire anyone who makes peace with themselves.

That was the thing about family.
Some people ran.
Some stayed bitter.
Some tried to meditate their way out of it.

My parents didn't talk about the old fights,
but I caught pieces—things that floated through the family:
"Said my wife wasn't good enough."
"She always thought she was better."
"You remember what she said at that wedding?"

It wasn't the content.
It was the weight.

Decades of passive-aggressive commentary turned into full-on radio
silence.
Eventually, people just stopped speaking.
Which meant I grew up not even knowing my relatives—let alone
bonding with them.

And when we moved to the U.S.?
The distance made it easier.
Out of sight, out of obligation.
No one called for Sunday chats.
No deep bonds to maintain.
We weren't leaving a tight-knit web.
We were weaving our own.

To their credit, my parents did the best they could.
Sure, they weren't emotional wizards.
They didn't teach us how to talk through feelings—or balance a checkbook.
But they raised us right.
With decency.

"Be kind.
Be honest.
Help people if you can.
Respect your elders—even when they don't deserve it."

They believed in goodness.
And that counts for something.

We weren't a *share your feelings* kind of family.
No long talks. Not much affection.

But they showed up.
They worked hard.
They took risks—so we wouldn't have to.

selective memory, selective ties

My mom grew up with four siblings.
I never got along with my grandfather on her side.

He was strict.
Ran the house with precision and zero patience—less father, more drill sergeant.

We fought all the time.
He thought my parents spoiled me—so he made it his mission to correct that.

Once, my parents gave me a purse—a gift.
Nothing extravagant, something they thought I'd like.
He snatched it away. Said I didn't deserve it.
Held it hostage, like he was delivering some grand lesson in humility.

But who was he to have a say?
The man who cheated on my grandmother—then left the maid everything when he died.
A man who always chose himself.

And in the end?
He didn't even remember any of it.
Because in his final days, he had Alzheimer's.

Didn't remember the betrayals, the hypocrisy, the way he tried to mold me into something smaller.

A lifetime of choices—good, bad, unforgivable—and then, *poof.*
Gone. Like a tape that unspooled, impossible to rewind.
Some memories stick. Others just... slip away.

His wife—my grandmother—the quieter one.
No harsh words. No defining moments.
Simply a presence.
Soft around the edges, like background music at a family gathering.

I try to remember her now,
but it's more of a feeling than a fact.

She wasn't loud. Didn't leave bold impressions.
She existed in the spaces between everyone else's chaos.

I guess that's another kind of forgetting—
not the kind that happens to you,
but the kind that happens to those left behind.

a grandfather's legacy
(or lack thereof)

My dad's family—eight siblings.
His mother? A force.
She raised all nine kids on her own after my grandfather died of a heart
attack at 57.

From what I've heard, he was cheating on her at the time—and died in
the middle of it.
Poetic justice? *Maybe.*

She never remarried.
Lived into her hundreds.
Strong. Half-deaf. Climbing stairs in her nineties.
Swore it was tofu.
Swatted my dad's hand away when he tried to carry her groceries.

"I'm not dead yet."

She wasn't the type to say *I love you.*
She served you food instead.
If love was measured in effort, she crushed it.

No meat. No shortcuts.
A lifetime of greens, tofu, and sheer willpower.

I like to think it went deeper than diet.
Stubbornness. Resilience.
Maybe even wisdom.
Or maybe she outlived the nonsense.

the few who stayed

When we moved to the States, we lost contact with most of our
relatives.
No family traditions. No group texts.
No birthday calls. No check-ins.
You can't lose what you never really had.

My sister and I reconnected with a few cousins over the years.
It helps that they live here.
Proximity kept the thread from unraveling.

Our parents have their favorites.
There's one sibling they call more than the others—the one who's
easiest to reach.
The default point of contact.
I used to wonder why.
Now I think: *At least someone's keeping a link alive.*

The older I get, the more I ask myself—what really makes a family?
Blood? Obligation? Shared history?
Or something else entirely?

Looking back, I don't see a traditional family. *Just fragments.*
Connections that came and went.
And somehow—my parents, my sister, and I—we made our own version.
Imperfect, but real.

Some people—the ones you share DNA with, the ones who *should* feel
like home—never do.
And some, with none of your blood, *somehow become your family.*

Maybe it's because the broken ones float toward each other.
Filling the gaps where real family failed us.
Shared trauma. Shared understanding.
Whatever it is, it runs deeper than DNA.

Some connections aren't inherited—they're chosen.
And honestly, those are the ones that matter most.

And yet, part of me wonders:
What if we'd been closer?
What if someone had reached out?
What if I had?
Would it have made a difference?

Some ties aren't meant to hold.
They stretch. They fray. They disappear.

But sometimes, you miss the idea.
Not the people exactly.
The idea.

The version where holidays are warm.
Conversations are easy.
And love doesn't come with a scorecard.

Even when you've created your own family—
your own home, your own rules—
that ache doesn't fully go away.

But the beauty of growing up is this:
Family isn't something you inherit.
It's defined—*by you.*

Through loyalty.
Through effort.
Through love that's *chosen*—not owed.

And if you're lucky?
You get to build it.
From scratch.
With people who show up.
Who stay.
Who speak your language—
even if it was never passed down.

the weight of silence

Silence carries weight—
especially in a family.
Not the peaceful kind—
the heavy kind.
Built from unspoken pain, unresolved fights,
years of swallowing what should've been said.

It's the tension that fills a room when everyone knows something's wrong
but acts like nothing is.
Fake normal. Forced smile.
The kind of quiet you choke on.

I grew up in that weight.
It crept into the walls,
into the space between us,
into *me.*

It wasn't all them.
At some point, I stopped trying too.
Stopped reaching through the walls they built—
and started building my own.

If I'd learned sooner how to say what I really felt—without fear of rejection or
misunderstanding—would it have changed anything?
Would I have been closer to the people I longed to reach?

Possibly.
But I'll never know.

Because distance becomes armor.
It keeps pain out—until it keeps everything out.
And in families, that kind of survival starts to feel like safety.
But it's not.

They say silence is golden.
But sometimes it's cowardice.
A way to avoid hard truths.
A way to keep the peace by pretending nothing ever broke.

It's not peace.
It's *rot*.

I used to romanticize blood.
Some bonds you're born into.
But the ones I built—*those* are the ones I trust.

Because avoidance doesn't mean resolution.
Sometimes it means we stopped trying to be understood.

falling into fallon

Fallon wasn't the plan. It was a plot twist.

nowhere, nevada

How my dad landed on Fallon—of all places—remains a mystery to me.
Anywhere else would've made more sense.
But this was it.
Middle of nowhere.
And somehow, it became ours.

If you've never heard of it—don't worry.
Most people haven't.
It's a small desert town, an hour east of Reno.
The kind of place where the air smells like alfalfa and dust.
Where tumbleweeds roll across the road like they're auditioning for an
old Western.

I remember the first time we pulled into town.
Dad behind the wheel, windows down,
my face sticky from melted candy and sibling squabbles stretched
across desert miles.
We stepped out, and the heat hit me like a wall.

Dry. Hot. Relentless.
Like the sky itself was pressing down on us.
Sagebrush.
Hot pavement.
The occasional whiff of manure from the nearby farms.

Seasons didn't change here—they ambushed you.
Blazing summers that stung your skin.
Winters so cold you had to warm up the car for ten minutes before
even thinking about driving.
Dry air that cracked your lips on contact.
Dust storms that swallowed the sky whole.

Some people thrive in that kind of climate.
I am not one of them.
Maybe that's why I ended up in California.

skates, sundaes & small-town rituals

Between the blistering summers and the teeth-chattering winters,
Fallon offered... creative outlets.

There was one movie theater in town.
Sticky floors, crackly speakers, and a half-lit marquee that flickered
like it had dreams of Vegas but settled for Fallon.

The Fallon Theatre had charm—if you squinted.
Red velvet seats that had seen better days,
a popcorn machine that never stopped rattling,
and a screen that hummed loud enough to compete with the dialogue.

I saw *Rocky IV* there as a kid, and when Apollo went down, I lost it.
Jumped out of my seat, popcorn flying, screaming at the screen like
Stallone could hear me: *Throw the towel, Rocky!*
Meanwhile, kids were making out in the back row like nothing happened.

Then there was Skate n Place—I think?
My personal kingdom.
Speed, rhythm, limbo champion status.
I laced up like it was showtime and rolled into the disco lights, music
blasting.
Hair in motion. Confidence in overdrive.
Every turn felt like freedom—like I was starring in my own music video.

Fallon also had a lake—Lahontan.
Technically outside of town, but close enough to count.
Some kids basically lived there all summer.

I'm not much of a water person.
If I can't see below me, I avoid it.
Tried water skiing once. Swallowed half the lake. Retired on the spot.
Also mistook a dead fish for a cool rock. *Still not over it.*

We had our spots.
The roller rink. The lake *(eh).*
The two streets we cruised like *The Fast and the Furious: Cornfield Drift.*

When we weren't doing laps, it was kegs by a bonfire.
Red Solo cups raised like it was church.
The highlight of a Friday night—and somehow, a social event.

Dating in Fallon was... limited.
Most people had already dated each other.
Sometimes it felt like everyone was taking turns.
If you weren't part of the rotation, you were either too picky—or too smart.

McDonald's was the beacon on Williams Avenue.
Big Macs to go. Parking lot chaos.
The apple pie was my go-to. Burned the roof of my mouth every time.
Still worth it.

Dairy Queen was the crown jewel.
Soft-serve swirls that could mend any bad day.
My order? A caramel sundae—extra caramel, neon cherry on top.

Cherry first. *It was law.*

Pizza Barn. The holy grail. Always.
Tucked in a strip mall, with a salad bar people actually trusted—
which, in Fallon, meant something.
Booths worn soft from birthdays and spilled sodas.
Walls lined with dusty trophies and faded team photos.

We celebrated everything there.
And we always fought over the last slice.
That crust? Crispy but chewy.
The melt? Gooey magic.
And the smell—molten cheese, browning pepperoni, rising dough—
it smelled like childhood.

But the real MVP?
My parents' restaurant.
More than a business. *It was home.*

The clatter of dishes. The sizzle of the wok.
My mom greeting regulars by name.
I remember doing homework at a corner booth—
the hum of conversation around me,
the aroma of garlic and soy sauce in the air.

It was the heartbeat of our family.
A place where food and love were served in equal measure.

the perks & pitfalls of belonging

Small towns come with small-town rules.
Everyone knows your business.
And being different? Meant being watched.

We were definitely different.

Asian in a town full of ranchers, farmers, and military families.
We stood out.
Add in the lifers—and yeah, we were an anomaly.

People butchered my name on the first day of school—every year.
Roll call was always a slow-motion train wreck.
Our last name? Sixteen letters. Never fit in the boxes.

Then we shortened it.
Sixteen letters to three.
A full identity haircut.

At the time, I told myself it was easier.
Less painful than correcting people every day.
But deep down, it felt like trimming a part of myself to fit.
A quiet loss no one noticed—but I carried it.

The original name sounded Thai.
Because for most of my childhood, that's what I thought I was.
Born in Thailand. Spoke Thai. Ate Thai food. Done.

Later I found out I was also Chinese.
Not from a family sit-down.
Thanks to 23andMe.
Huh.

Both my parents were ethnically Chinese—born and raised in Thailand.
So technically I'm Chinese, born in Thailand, raised in America.
A walking Venn diagram.

No wonder people were confused. *I* was confused.
Sometimes I still am.

"Wait, so... are you Thai or Chinese?"
Yes. Final answer.

That question used to rattle me—like I was supposed to pick a side.
But the older I got, the more I realized—
I'm not split. I'm stacked.
Layered like a cultural parfait.
Thai. Chinese. American.
All of it. At once.

Some were curious. Others assumed.
And when you're quiet, people aren't sure how to approach you.

Sometimes we were invisible.
Sometimes we were a spectacle.

But rarely just... regular.

It took time—but we found our rhythm.
My parents made friends.
Regulars turned into chosen family.

My sister and I found our own crew, bit by bit.
A few awkward lunch breaks, a group project or two... eventually,
something stuck.
There weren't lightning-strike friendships.
Mostly small, quiet connections that added up:
a shared laugh in class.
someone saving me a seat at lunch.
A note passed during science with a dumb doodle.
Small moments. But real.
And sometimes, that's all it takes.

In the end, it wasn't about blending in.
It was about staying.
Becoming part of the backdrop—and then, somehow, part of the story.

Slowly, Fallon became more than a pit stop.

We even started waving back at people.
The *two-finger steering wheel wave?*
That's when I knew we were no longer visitors.
We were *Fallon-ized.*

final thought: the place
that raised me

Feeling at home doesn't announce itself.
No grand gesture. No spotlight.
It just... happens.

One day, you're the "Wait—how do you say your name again?" girl.
Next? You're giving directions on Main Street.
The bank teller asks how your parents are—by name.
Someone spots you in the grocery store and waves like they've known
you forever.

You're no longer passing through.
You've got roots—even if they're new.
Even if they don't go that deep.

We started belonging—
not because we blended in,
but because we stayed.

Even in Fallon, I kept translating:
between cultures, expectations,
even the version of me I thought they wanted to see.

Fallon raised me.
Not in a warm, fuzzy, postcard kind of way—

but in the way a place seeps into your bones.
The way it humbles you.
Hardens you.
Then softens you.

It gave me dust storms and Dairy Queen,
dead fish and dance recitals,
mismatched friendships and a taste of what it means
to stand out—and stand firm anyway.

It challenged me.
Shaped me.
Taught me how to belong without disappearing.

And no matter where I go next,
some dusty, sunburned little piece of me will always belong to it.

Against all odds.
And probably against my will.

Fallon didn't ask me to belong.
It simply waited to see if I'd stay.

✦

fashion as a religion

"Fashion is the armor to survive the reality of everyday life." —Bill
Cunningham

dress like you mean it

Looking the part wasn't free.
It cost me silence, spirals, and more wardrobe changes than a
Vegas showgirl.
And sometimes, the crash after the serve was louder than the applause.

My first fashion memory? Red jelly sandals.
I was maybe five. *Obsessed.*
Shiny. Plastic. Glittery perfection. Technically reserved for special
occasions.
But I wore them everywhere, mesmerized by how they caught the light.

It wasn't about being pretty.
It was about being seen—on my own terms.
That's when I realized: even shoes could hold power.
Even if they lit the room up with every squeaky step.

At thirteen, that knowing deepened.
I walked into school in a cropped Guess jacket.
Heads turned.
For once, I was the one in control.

I had a rule: if someone else wore the same shirt, it was dead to me.
Banished to the fashion graveyard.
Standing out wasn't optional—it was survival.

Two style saints wired my DNA: Madonna and Prince.
Not to *be* them—to be *that* free.

Madonna in that polka-dot blouse with the giant ruffle?
Done for.
She wasn't dressed—she was daring.
Flirty but untouchable.
She made you look—and *want* to be looked at.
I didn't just want that blouse. I wanted the *audacity*.

And Prince?
A walking masterclass in defiance and glam.
Lace, ruffles, heeled boots.
He didn't care. He didn't ask. *He declared.*

Watching him, I understood—fashion wasn't decoration.
It was language. A weapon. A full-blown identity.
No words required.

braces, glasses, hair: transformations

Some kids begged for a puppy.
In eighth grade, I begged for braces.

I saw the future, and it was grim—high school photos with an
overbite, a front gap, teeth fighting for position.
So I campaigned. Hard.
Flashed my chaotic little smile in the mirror, sighed dramatically, made
sure my parents knew: this was a full-blown orthodontic emergency.

And it worked.

Weeks later, I was sentenced to two years of metal mouth.
At first, I felt victorious.
Then came the pain. The wax. The rubber bands.
My glow-up era had officially begun—and immediately backfired.

And then there was my hair.
Not an accessory—*a mood ring*. It changed constantly.
One day: voluminous curls.
The next: stick-straight with a part sharp enough to cut glass.

I had eras:
The perm phase *(volume = power)*.
The shaved-on-one-side, curly-on-the-other look *(don't ask)*.
The low ponytail with one rogue curl down the back *(why??)*.

Whatever the phase, it always came back to identity.

Some days I'd spend three, maybe four hours on my hair.
Crimp, curl, tease—sealed with enough Aqua Net to ruin the ozone.
It was thick. Dramatic. Over-styled to the heavens.
People asked if it was a wig.
Not a wig. Just commitment—plus a dash of delusion.

Then came the dyeing. The re-dyeing. The breaking point.
Until I tried to lighten it... and my hair started falling out.

So I grabbed scissors.
Weirdly liberating.

There's a reason they say we hold emotions in our hair.
When I started cutting, it wasn't split ends I was shedding—
it was fear.
Control.
The pressure to be pretty.

Maybe that's what led to the buzzcut years.
When I finally ditched the hair entirely and let my face take center stage.
No smoke. No mirrors. No crimping required.

It was terrifying.
It was thrilling.
For once—the reflection *honest.*

the gospel according to vogue

Some kids had a Bible on their nightstand.
I had *Vogue*.

Glossy pages. High drama.
Fashion editorials that felt like fairy tales—
tulle, leather, backcombed hair, impossible shoes.

I didn't flip through it—I studied it.
Each issue was scripture.
Every photo, a sermon.
Every model, a prophet.

They weren't just pretty.
They were powerful.

I sat on my bed, flipping through *Seventeen, Vogue, Teen*—
tearing out pages that mattered.
Vogue gave me high-fashion dreams.
Seventeen taught me what was cool right now.
Teen had celebrity crushes—
but I came for the clothes.

The pages covered my walls like gospel:
oversized blazers, lace gloves, polka dots with attitude,
leather that meant business.

And then—Benetton hit like a lightning bolt.
Every image was a map to some brighter, freer version of myself.
Vibrant colors. Diverse faces.
Models styled like they belonged to some beautiful, unruly world
I hadn't been invited to.

It wasn't just fashion.
It was a message.
Loud. Fearless. Inclusive.
They weren't selling sweaters.
They were selling belonging.

No edits. No disclaimers. No dimming the lights.

And I bought it—hook, line, neon-striped sinker.
Like someone cracked open the world and whispered,
You belong here. Loud colors and all.
Even if Fallon didn't get the memo.

I'd stare at those spreads for hours—memorizing poses,
imagining what it felt like to live inside that frame.
Dog-ear the corners. Cut them out. Tape them up—
a vision board before I even knew the term.

It was aspirational.
But also strangely... attainable.
Maybe I could borrow a little of that magic.
Maybe I could become someone people looked at—
the way I looked at them.

In a town where everyone wore the same jeans
and anything too out-there got side-eyed at the lunch table,
fashion became my quiet rebellion.
My armor.
My escape.

By high school, I wasn't just following trends—
I was ahead of them.

That McDonald's cat watch from a Happy Meal? A statement.
The velvet turquoise jacket from Contempo Casuals? An obsession.
Limited-edition sneaker drops? Already on my radar.

Fashion wasn't about fitting in.
It was my filter, my forcefield, my quiet rebellion.

A middle finger in silk—tailored, pressed, and ready.

look, serve, compete

It wasn't only about the clothes. Or the hair.
Let's be real—I was *serving*.

One day it clicked: cropped Guess jacket, matching faded denim cuffed
right, crisp white sneakers.
I walked into school and—for the first time—I didn't show up. I *owned*
the hallway.

There were no days off.
Getting dressed wasn't routine—it was ritual.

Pick the outfit. Check the mirror.
Pose once—for me.
Pose again—in case someone's watching.
School. Gas station. Roller rink—I stayed ready.

"You're really going for it, huh?" someone said, smirking.
I took it as a compliment.
Because yeah—I was.

High school brought bigger stages—and higher stakes.
Dance wasn't about movement. It was competition.
And fashion? Part of the routine.
Part armor. Part performance.

Rehearsals had a look.
Competitions had a vibe.
Costumes? Full-blown transformations.
We weren't just showing up. We were *becoming*.

Backstage throbbed with nerves and glitter.
Hairspray clouds. Lashes clinging to mirrors.
Someone crying over a lost earring.
Someone else hot-gluing rhinestones like their life depended on it.

Some girls fixed their makeup.
Others whispered pep talks into the mirror—*conjuring courage through eyeliner.*

I had my own prep:
Shoes tied just right—then tied again.
A specific lipstick. Lucky scrunchie. Charm bracelet.
Once, even a mini can of glitter hairspray.

Fashion was my superpower—even in dance.
It was how I walked into a room and said: *I'm ready.*

It wasn't about nailing the eight-count alone.
It was about *owning* the moment.
Every rhinestone. Every perfectly placed bobby pin.
All part of the story I was telling—without saying a word.

laughing in leopard

Not every look landed.

One day, I wore a leopard-print faux fur coat to school.
Thrifted. Slightly too big. Absolutely fabulous.
Black leggings. Scuffed white high-tops.
A red lip I probably wasn't allowed to wear.

I walked in like I owned the place—confident, electric, *loud on purpose.*
Until someone snickered in the hallway.
Then another.

By lunch, I was questioning everything.
Maybe it was too much.
Maybe *I* was too much.
(*Still cute*, for the record.)

But then it hit me—
So what if they laughed?
At least they noticed.
I'd rather be unforgettable than palatable.
Seen, not safe.

After I buzzed my hair, people really didn't know what to do with me.
I got sir'd at least twice a week.
People assumed I was a lesbian. Or in the military.

Or mourning something. Or mid-breakdown.

My haircut became a Rorschach test—
their projections said more about them than me.

Funny thing?
I got hit on more after the cut.
By men.
Go figure.

Just the other day, my boyfriend and I were out to dinner.
After we paid, the owner yelled after us:
"Come back again, boys!"
We lost it.
Mistaken identity?
We'll take it.

Or yesterday—at a café when a guy chased me into the parking lot.
Said he liked women with short hair who look like tomboys.
Then asked if he could take me out.

Um... no, thanks.
Sounds like a you problem.

At some point, you stop correcting people.
You just let them show you who they are.

I didn't need decoding anymore.
Let 'em guess.
I already knew who I was.

style as identity
(and the work it covered)

As I got older, the stakes changed—
but the strategy didn't.

Birthday party. Nineteen-some-time ago.
Iconic Union Club on the Sunset Strip.
Gucci bustier. Men's underwear. Leather trench. Stilettos.
Pencil-thin eyebrows. A full face. Confidence on 100.
Absurd. Fabulous. *Intentional.*

And yeah—I smoked back then.
Someone once told me it might *deepen* my voice.
I had this soft, mousy tone, and a dancer friend swore a little gravel
would give me more presence.
Did it work? *Who knows.*
But in the moment, it felt like part of the character I was becoming.

Everything I wore was a message—louder, sharper, *impossible to ignore.*

And it worked.
People noticed.
Rooms tilted.
Eyes landed on me.
And for a second, it felt amazing.
Powerful.

Exactly what I'd worked for,
even if sometimes only I could read it.

Then came the quiet questions:
Did they see *me*—or just the outfit?
Did they like the *shine?* Or were they just *squinting?*
Was I *misrepresenting* myself?

The look said *power.*
The truth said: *figuring it out.*

The outside had arrived.
The inside was trying to keep up.
It wasn't just expression.
It was a *mask* I'd learn to wear.

Eventually, I had to ask:
Was it *protecting* me...
presenting me...
or *hiding* me?

seen, but not chosen

"How certainty gets read as rejection.
How untouchable girls... don't get touched."

There was a rumor I'd been voted Best Body in high school—
maybe it was a joke, maybe hallway lore—
but it stuck.

And what a strange thing to be known for.
Not smartest. Not kindest.
Just: *that.*

Was I supposed to be proud? Grateful?
It felt less like a compliment, more like a trophy labeled *Most Stared At.*
Like my body was public property—up for vote, up for grabs.

A guy once wrote in my yearbook:
"Good luck at UNLV and keep dancing great with that totally awesome
body God gave you. Put those jugs to good use. Love, Darren."

Another:
"You're hot, but scary. Good luck out there."
Gee. Thanks, Travis. *Inspirational stuff.*

And Ronnie:

"I wish we could've gone to prom together. I think it would have been most *unprecidented*." (His spelling, not mine.)

"Oh well, maybe we could do something to make up for that…"

Sweet. Awkward.
Probably the closest anyone ever got to actually asking.

I was slowly growing into it—
into a body that got watched, measured, mythologized.
All without consent.

Sounded like flattery.
Felt like branding.

And the kicker?
No one ever asked me to a dance.
No prom. No homecoming.
Not even Sadie Hawkins.

No corsage. No cheesy photo to cringe at later.
Only a strange absence where a rite of passage should've been.

I told myself I was too intimidating. Too focused on dance. *Too something.*
Years later, I asked a guy friend why.

He shrugged.
"Because no one wants to get turned down," he said.
Said he wanted to—thought I'd say no.

And that floored me.

I wasn't cold.
I was scared, too.

But under hallway lights,
confidence looked like a fortress.

And no one taught me how to lower the drawbridge.

final thought:
fashion as a first language

Before I found my voice, I found my style.
Before I knew who I was, I knew how I *wanted* to be seen.

It started as protection.
Became performance.
Turned into power.

Fashion was my first language.
My first *yes*.
My first rebellion.

It made me feel seen—*even when I didn't know what I was looking for.*

The outside showed up first—loud and certain.
The inside took its time.

But somewhere in the layers—the styling, the staging—
it became something real.
Stitched with intention.
Worn like truth.

Before anyone told me I was beautiful,
I'd already decided I was.

✦

wok, lipstick & grit

The American Dream came in red, white, and fine print.

a restaurant named chinatown

My parents opened a Chinese restaurant and named it *Chinatown*.
Original, I know. Somehow, it fit.
School, home, restaurant—repeat.

The first location was tiny.
We lived right above it—the fridge's hum was our unofficial
soundtrack.
Cramped. Loud. Always in motion.

But business picked up. Lines stretched. Takeout orders stacked high.
We moved into a bigger building. Same heart. More room to breathe.

It wasn't some dim sum palace—no golden dragons, no red lacquered
walls.
Before my parents took over, it was a *Country Kitchen*—meatloaf, eggs,
coffee at sunrise.
Honestly? It *still* had the vibe.
Brown vinyl booths. Wood-paneled walls.
No remodel—just a new name and a better menu.
Same bones. New story.
Didn't need flash. *It had flavor.*

Our lives moved to the rhythm of the kitchen clock.
It was more than a place we worked.
It was *home.*

The sounds of my dad yelling and my mom responding weren't
arguments—they were choreography.
A different kind of language—timing, heat, and grind.

You could hear it before stepping inside:
the hiss of steam, the chop of cleavers, metal spatulas scraping the flat-top.
And the smells? You could follow them from the parking lot.

Fried rice—sizzling, savory, perfectly charred.
Egg rolls—crisp outside, steam inside.
Sweet and sour pork—my dad's signature dish. Tangy. Balanced.
Addictive.
I've never tasted one quite like his.

That scent clung to us—in our clothes, our hair, our skin.
Followed me from grade school to grown.

I didn't chop. Didn't stir.
But I stood tall when my friends walked in—like I *owned* the place.
Especially when they walked in.

They raved about the food.
Begged their parents to bring them back.
Bragged that they knew the owners.
They loved my parents, too.
They saw what I saw: two people pouring everything they had into
something solid. Not flashy. Not trendy. *Real.*

And when customers thanked them—*really* thanked them—you could see:
My parents weren't proud of the business alone.
They were proud of the work. The food. The care.

They weren't only serving meals.
They were serving *meaning.*

I didn't know it then,
but I was soaking it *all in.*

the kitchen & the crew

My dad was a legit chef.
No cooking school. No formal training.
Just instinct, heat, and a sharp knife.
He said he learned while working at a restaurant in college.
Why New Mexico? No one really knew. That part never fully added up.
But somehow, between textbooks and side gigs, he learned to cook.
All his recipes? His own.

His work ethic? Ruthless.
He ran the kitchen like a battlefield commander—barking orders,
sleeves rolled up, head down.
No shortcuts. No excuses. Get it done.
I admired him.
Feared him a little, too.
That kind of intensity leaves an imprint.

Lucky was Dad's right-hand man.
The sous chef. The steady hand when things got wild.
I don't think that was his real name—more like one of those
nicknames that sticks.
Maybe Dad gave it to him. Maybe he gave it to himself.
Either way, he was Lucky.

No yelling. No ego. Just quiet precision.
He moved like he carried his own gravity—unbothered,

unflustered, unshakable.
When the heat cranked up, I'd drift toward Lucky—he made it bearable.

Then there was Don.
Dishwasher. Busser. Backup cook. Utility player of the highest order.
I think he was Native—probably from the nearby reservation.
Quiet guy. Gentle eyes. The sweetest soul.
Always showed up. Never made a fuss. Got to work.

Except... he liked to drink.
Some nights, he came in off.
Glassy eyes. Heavy steps.
The kind of tired sleep can't fix.

My parents noticed.
Pulled him aside. Firm but kind.
No yelling. No threats.
Simply: *We see you. But this has to change.*

And to his credit, it did.
He cleaned up. Came in early. Stayed late.
Same Don, but steadier. Sober.

You could see the difference—in his pace, in his smile.
Not a big announcement. A quiet transformation.
A man showing up for himself the same way he showed up for us.

I think about him sometimes.
Wonder where he ended up.
If he's okay.
If he stayed on that straighter path.

Because he was a good guy.
The kind you root for.
The kind you hope life was finally kind to.

The kitchen was chaos.
But inside it?
They taught me how to hold steady in the fire.

Especially my dad.
The more I watched him cook,
the more I wondered about *everything he wasn't saying*.

a past wrapped in silence

My dad's cooking was loud.
Bold flavors. Big presence.
But when I asked about his past? Nothing.

Not cold. Not angry. Completely... sealed.

Where did you learn to cook?
Why New Mexico?
Why Chinese food?

The answers varied, day to day.
One version: college job, picked it up fast, never stopped.
Another: learned back in Thailand.
Maybe a friend. Maybe no one.

None of it quite lined up.
And when I pressed, he'd pivot—homework, errands, a quick subject
change.

I used to think it was forgetfulness.
Now I think it was self-protection.
He didn't want to go back.
Or maybe he didn't know how.

Asian parents don't always share.
Not because they don't love you—
because *survival was the answer.*

What matters is that we're here.
The lights are on. The food is hot.
The rest? Doesn't need to be discussed.

Still, I searched.
Listened for clues.
Connected dots that barely existed.
Always wondering.

What made him that way?
So driven. So closed off?
Maybe I'll never know.
Maybe he doesn't remember.
Or maybe he remembers too much—
and doesn't want me to carry it.

But one thing was clear:
Whatever he lived through,
he turned into a life.
A reputation.
Plates people still talk about.

No stories. No explanations.
The kind you could taste.
The kind that lingers.

For him? That was enough.

I didn't realize it then,
but I'd carry that sealed space too—
in my own voice, in my own chapters.

the front of the house:
queen of composure

If my dad was fire,
my mom was the calm.
Out front—smiling, focused, precise.
A quiet kind of command.

She ran the dining room like a maître d' with a sixth sense.
Knew which customers wanted extra chili paste,
which needed their tea refilled without asking.
Knew when to pause, when to float, when to disappear.

She didn't fawn. Didn't fake it.
But people felt taken care of.
Seen, even if they didn't know why.

The military guys called her "ma'am" and treated her like royalty.
Regulars knew her by name, brought small gifts, shared stories about
their grandkids.

It looked effortless.
Maybe it came from her old airline days—working the *Lufthansa*
counter at the Bangkok airport.
Jet-lagged travelers. Impatient businessmen. Screaming toddlers.
She'd smile through all of it. Trained for chaos.
Trained to stay calm when people were at their worst.

Or maybe she was built that way—cool, capable, magnetic.
The kind of presence people trusted instantly.

That's how she met my dad.
He worked there too. Asked her out.
She said no. Then no again.
Persistent—that was my dad.

Eventually, she said yes.
That one yes became everything—a business, a family, a life.

I used to watch her from the host stand—
knee-length skirt, blouse tucked in, belt perfectly cinched.
Estée Lauder Classic Red on her lips.
Composed. Unmistakably her.

She made people feel seen—without giving too much away.
Soft—but never small.

Some male customers flirted.
She didn't notice.
But I did.

I saw how they looked at her—misreading kindness for invitation.
It made me cringe.
Made me want to yell: *Back off.*

But she never reacted.
Never lost her cool.

She was damn good at it.
The kind of good that stays with you—
that teaches you how to hold a room without raising your voice.

She held the room like a pro.

translator in training

My sister actually worked.
Took orders. Bussed tables. Ran food.
I floated in like a guest star—smiling, handing out menus,
waving at regulars like I was running for office,
then vanishing to the back with a Shirley Temple and a plate of egg rolls.

Wasn't lazy.
Didn't see the restaurant as my path.
Didn't see myself in the hustle.
Not like that.

Turns out, I wasn't built for the trenches.
I was wired for the stories—
the noticing, the remembering, the turning it all into something that
made sense.
Or so I told myself.

I had my uses.
Sometimes I'd translate—
bridge what my parents meant and what the diners needed.
A menu question here. A phone call there.
Nothing major. But helpful.

And in hindsight?
That was the start of something.

Not in the kitchen—
in communication.
Translation. Connection.

Because when you grow up interpreting for your parents,
you learn to read people.
Smooth over confusion with a smile.
Speak for others before you even know how to speak for yourself.

I didn't stir the pot.
I narrated it.

Then came the golden shift.
I smiled, said maybe three words,
and walked away with a crisp fifty-dollar bill.

Fifty bucks—for what?
Being adorable?

My parents were running on steam and stress.
I was cashing in on dimples.

I waited for someone to say:
Oops. Mistake.

But no. It was mine.
Best shift of the decade.
Easiest money I ever made.

Honestly?
I peaked early.

our one-day escape

No matter how busy the restaurant got,
my parents made sure of one thing—
we always had one day off.
Non-negotiable. Sacred. Ours.

One day a week when the restaurant stayed dark,
the woks went cold,
and my parents did something rare—
they let someone else cook for them.

We'd pile into the car and drive.
Didn't matter where.
A new city. A new hole-in-the-wall.
Some place my dad read about, some menu my mom wanted to decode.
It wasn't only about eating—
it was about discovery. Escape. Breathing room.

We had a ritual.
Whenever we passed a hay truck—those giant semis stacked high with
golden bales—we'd yell in unison, like it was law:
"Hay hay! Bale of hay! Make a wish and turn away!"

Then we'd snap our heads to the side, eyes shut,
wishes swirling like whipped cream in a milkshake.
I don't know where it came from—

maybe we made it up, maybe we stole it.
But we believed, in that kid way,
that if we played it right, our wishes might come true.

And for those few seconds, we were in it together.
Voices echoing, tires humming, a wish hanging in the air.

When we turned back—hay truck gone, moment passed—
it was like we'd done something right.
Like we'd sent a tiny secret into the universe and trusted it to find its way.

Even now, if I pass a hay truck on the 101 or 405,
some deep part of me still wants to shout it.
Still wants to make a wish.
It was silly. It was weird.
It was *ours.*

And that one day a week—away from orders and ovens—
we weren't a restaurant family.
We were a family.

While my parents studied menus like national secrets,
I ran silent investigations at the surrounding tables.

The couple not speaking? Mid-divorce. Or mid-standoff.
The guy in cargo shorts with three iced teas and a Bluetooth? Pyramid
scheme. Mafia. Possibly both.
The woman sipping chardonnay at noon? Icon. Mistress. Life coach.
All of the above.

I crafted full-blown sagas between buffet runs—
crab legs, shrimp cocktail, enough garlic butter to drown a secret.
Love affairs. Petty grudges. Dramatic walkouts—I had *range*.

I didn't know it then,
but that was my first storytelling workshop.
Give me a booth at the Peppermill seafood buffet and five minutes of
awkward body language, and I'd give you three-act structure.

Turns out, I wasn't just observing—
I was *rehearsing*.

an education without knowing it

The restaurant wasn't the only thing I inherited.
I got the radar, too.

It never felt like school—
but that's exactly what it was.
Not math. Not science.
Something more useful:
how to dine, notice, read a room.

How to scan a menu like a pro.
Feel the energy the second you walk in.
Clock whether the staff had it together.

I watched my mom—how she carried herself, how she silently read
the room: folded napkins, food temp, pacing of the meal.

In our world, details mattered.
The plating. The presentation. The timing.
It all spoke—effort, care, pride.

Maybe that's why I care so much now.
The look. The service.
The feeling before the first bite.

Whether it's fashion, food, or design—
packaging shows you how much someone cared.

Those meals were more than food.
They were about presence.
No distractions. No orders piling up.
Just us. A table.
Time that felt slower. Softer. Full.

One day a week, we weren't working.
We were living.

Even now, when I walk into a restaurant, I feel it—
that quiet current of care.

The way a glass is placed.
The pause between courses.
The unspoken rhythm between kitchen and floor.

It's not about *fancy*.
It's about *intention*.

And without knowing it,
I was learning to read what wasn't said.
To recognize effort.
To notice love, disguised as detail.

That kind of education stays with you.
Long after the meal is over.
In everything you create.
In everything you choose.

final thought: what stuck with me

You'd think—growing up in a restaurant with a chef for a father—I'd
know my way around a wok.
That I'd be slicing, dicing, stir-frying like a pro.
Nope.

But dining out? That was my lane.
The flavors. The service. The energy of a space.
It was never about the food alone.
It was how it all came together.

Those weekly outings weren't just breaks from the grind.
They were blueprints.

I've seen the other side—
the pressure, the prep, the sweat behind every plate.
How much care can live in something small—
something gone in a few bites.

It taught me:
Love lives in the doing, not only the saying.

And drilled one thing deep into my bones—
how you do anything is how you do everything.

The restaurant didn't have a runway.
But it had rhythm.
A flow.
A front-of-house performance that taught me timing, delivery,
and the art of making someone feel seen.
Like my mom did.
Like Lucky did.
Like Don did.

I didn't always get it.
But some of my dad's fire—his precision, his pace—
got into me too.

I may not have held a knife.
But I inherited his drive.

All that attention to detail—
how something looked, how it moved—
wasn't turning me into a diner.

It was turning me into someone who could read the room.
Feel the pulse.
Know when to turn up the heat.

And serve it—hot, clean, intentional—
before it ever hit the plate.

It was shaping me into a storyteller.
One with taste.

✦

the yes years

Joy takes practice.
We started out small.
We said yes.

when we could

We could.
And we did.

That was the turning point.
From hoping to knowing.
From survival to stability.

Family day trips had a rhythm—and shopping was part of it.
My sister and I knew: if we went, we were coming home with
something new.
Shoes. A sweater. A jacket we didn't need.
Sometimes, I didn't even like what I picked out.
The point was—we could.

And when you've lived with just enough, even small things feel enormous.

There was comfort in the transaction.
It wasn't about the clothes.
It was about what it meant.
We're okay now.

A ritual. A reset.
Retail therapy as sacrament.
The hush of a dressing room.

The crinkle of bags in the backseat.
Whispered: *You're safe now.*

As business grew, so did we.
The buffet. The Thai place. The steakhouse.
Each one a risk that worked.

We moved from living above the restaurant
to a mobile home with plastic chandeliers and golden faucets,
then a real house on Moody Lane.
Four bedrooms. Three bathrooms.
Real furniture—the kind you picked, not inherited.

Our fridge had options.
So did our lives.

That house was freedom.
Downstairs was mine—mirrored studio, dance dojo.
To my parents, it meant more than a win.
It was proof.
The double shifts. The 18-table weekends.
It all added up.

They didn't want flash—
they wanted future.
A life no one could take away.

Even the silence felt luxurious.
No clanging dishes. No ringing phones.
The quiet *felt earned*—
a house that finally exhaled.

And then came the cars.

My dad had a thing about cars.
Mileage. Make. Status.

First: the burgundy Cadillac.
Sleek. Heavy. Full of I've-made-it energy.
Then the Mercedes era—three confusingly identical models.
After that:
Jeep Grand Cherokee
Ford Expedition
Ford Bronco
F-150 (hauled zero things)
Land Rover (...Nevada off-roading?)
And finally—the camper.

That camper was the dream.
"We'll take family road trips," he said.
But it never left the driveway.

Sunbaked. Patient.
Waiting to be invited on a grand adventure.
That journey never came.
But the dream sat there, parked in plain sight.

Vacations were rare. Business came first.
But when they happened? Magic.
The Grand Canyon. Yosemite. Lake Tahoe.
And once—Salt Lake City.

We were driving my sister to the Air Force Academy—for her first year.
Somewhere in Utah, I fell asleep in the backseat.
My dad stopped for gas.
I slipped out to use the bathroom.

When I came back—the car was gone.

No dad. No car.
Only me.
Utah. Parking lot. Panic.

Full meltdown.
Sobbing.
This was it—my milk carton moment.

Twenty minutes later, he came tearing back in.
Eyes wide. Hands shaking.
He thought I was still asleep—until he checked the mirror.

He called my mom right away.
She dropped the shaker mid-shift, screamed in Thai,
swore her heart stopped.

At the time, it was terrifying.
Now? It's a classic.

A family legend.
Told with mock horror, dramatic flair, and just enough exaggeration
to make it worth it.
Not because we forgot the fear—
but because we survived it.

Those years were sacred. And silly.
Every purchase meant more.
Every trip became a story.
Even the camper became part of the mythology.

And through it all, my sister stayed steady.
Unshaken. Unbothered. Untouchable.
You never knew what she was feeling—
and that was the point.

Still face. Locked vault.
While I was the chaos—
the spark, the sob, the storm—
she was the eye of it.

Not loud. Not showy. Not interested in being understood.
But she stayed.
Always.

That was her version of love.
Not soft.
But solid.

kindness as currency

We weren't the only ones—
my parents were generous with everyone.
Friends got invited to dinners, day trips, shopping sprees.
And when the bill came, it was always a tug-of-war.

I watched my dad fake a bathroom break—
just to swipe his card first.
Next time, my mom did the same.
A silent competition:
who could pay faster, sneakier, first.
Generosity as blood sport.

My mom's version looked different.
She sent everyone home with food—
staff, friends, even my classmates.

The restaurant became our ritual.
We'd pile into a corner booth, pretend to study,
and inhale whatever was hot and ready.
The restaurant bustled,
but we had our own world carved out in the middle of it.

Once we were full—and a little high on soy sauce and sugar—
we'd head to the back lot for dodgeball.
No teams. No rules.

And then—chaos.
Someone always got whacked in the face.
The kitchen clanged.
Our laughter bounced off the concrete.

Full bellies.
A grease-stained lot.
Freedom.

In our world, picking up the check wasn't just kindness.
It was pride.
A quiet flex.
Proof we'd made it—
not because we said so,
but because we didn't flinch when it came time to give.

Looking back, it wasn't about the Cadillac,
the steakhouse,
or a closet full of clothes.
It was about the *feeling.*

We stopped chasing it.
Started living it—messy, beautiful, ours.

I didn't know I was learning.
The reflex to offer? That's muscle memory.
It's probably why I still tip big.
Why I always bring extra.
Why I ask *Do you need anything?*—and actually mean it.

We gave because we could.
Not just with money—but with meaning.
Every extra plate. Every open door.
Love you didn't have to earn.

✦

no curtain call

Didn't win. Still iconic.

from the restaurant to the real world

The curtain didn't rise right away.
Life did.

By high school, something clicked.
I'd learned how to perform—
not on stage, but in life.
Maybe it was leftover middle school defiance.
Or the restaurant—teaching me to read people, spot danger, charm strangers.
Or maybe it was time.

High school: louder. Bigger.
More pressure. More performance.
Suddenly, everything mattered.

How you dressed. Who you sat with. What you did after school.
The safety of my middle school bubble? Gone.
This was a new game.

Freshman year, I was a small fish in a crowded pond.
The moment I stepped on campus, it hit me:
The seniors weren't just older—they were a different species.
Taller. Cooler.
Small-town legends in letterman jackets—iconic.

Couples held hands like they were married, making out in broad daylight.
Effortless. Confident.
Meanwhile, I was trying to figure out where to stand.
How to walk. Where to sit.

Somewhere between classes, I spotted my sister in the hall.
She moved with her crew—easy, poised, like they owned the place.
And they did.

For her, high school was familiar.
For me? A reboot.
No map. No script.
Just a hallway full of strangers and the quiet panic of not knowing
who to be.

I needed something to anchor me.
A role to play.
So I smiled my way onto the cheer team.

I never knew the actual plays,
but I could shout on cue.
I smiled big. Jumped high.
Moved like I belonged.

But inside, I was holding my breath.
Working to earn a place.
Passing as someone who wasn't unraveling.

I didn't feel cool or popular.
I felt like I was cosplaying someone who did—
and praying no one could see through it.

high school: the rebel awakens

The good girl act was cracking.
Not a full break—just enough to catch the light.
Missed assignments. Skipped class.
Eye rolls that lingered too long.

Then I stopped pretending.
Started ditching school.
Left at lunch and didn't come back.
Found the kids who didn't care and made it a lifestyle.
Tested every limit—then blew right past them.

One day I snapped at my English teacher.
She said something—I don't even remember what.
But it hit a nerve.
And before I could stop myself:
"Bitch."
Right there. In class.

The room froze.
Because I wasn't that kid.
I was the one who turned in homework.
The one teachers liked.
The one who never talked back.

Even the principal looked confused.
Her? Really?

But yeah.
Really.

No one could stand that teacher.
Everyone had a story—
the sighs, the power trips. Brutal.
So when I said it, it felt like I took one for the team.
Said what everyone else was too scared to.

And it felt good.
Like a wire had been cut.
The act? Over.
The edge? Finally out.

And it didn't stop.

Halftime—drinking Purple Passion under the bleachers.
Still in uniform. Still cheering like I wasn't falling apart.
Couldn't hold my liquor.
Threw up behind the snack shack.
Like a PSA gone wrong.

Thus began the legend of *Purple Passion Puker.*
Everyone laughed—
even me.

Until the joke got old. *And I was still the punchline.*

the slide into chaos

Detention.
More ditching.
I was slipping further through the cracks.

And then—the party.

Junior year.
My parents were visiting my sister at college, which meant one thing:
An empty house. Open season.

It started innocent—a few friends, a night to ourselves.
What I didn't count on? The liquor stash.
Unlocked. Abundant. Waiting.

Drinks flowing. Voices rising. Boundaries blurring.
Then someone backed a truck into a tree.
Not a bump—a crack.
The kind of hit you can't talk your way out of.

Cue panic. Cue headlights. Cue the sheriff at the door.

I opened it—heart pounding, face calm.
Pennies in my mouth—someone swore it sobered you up.
(It doesn't. It's metallic regret.)

I mumbled something.
Somehow, they didn't take us in.
But the damage was done.

My parents found out.
I had to confess.
Not my finest hour—but not my lowest.

Because not long after that—I got arrested.

It started small.
A drugstore candy bar turned into a slow-motion crime spree.
To see if I could.
I could.
Then I did it again.
Not for the stuff—for the thrill.
The invisible dare.
The quiet power of walking out clean.

I didn't need any of it.
My parents gave me everything.
If I wanted something, I had it.
So why was I stealing?

Control?
Attention?
Proximity to the edge?

Maybe I wanted to get caught.

Because when you have everything, people assume you need nothing.

But I did.
I needed to be seen.
Not for my grades. Not for being fine.
(For the mess underneath.)

I wasn't stealing things.
I was trying to be heard—without having to explain myself.

What started small turned into clothes. Jewelry. Makeup.
Not harmless anymore.
Each clean exit fed the next.
Each getaway felt like proof that I was untouchable.

Until Macy's.

I don't remember everything I took.
But I remember the weight.
Not in my bag—in my gut.
I knew.
(I had pushed too far.)

Still, I walked out.
Still thought I'd won.

Until two undercover cops grabbed me—one on each arm.
Firm. Immediate. No escape.

The handcuffs clicked before I could process it.
I wasn't a rebel anymore—just a teenage girl in the back of a cop car.

It was official.

the aftermath: the weight
of disappointment

Sitting in that cold, fluorescent-lit holding room,
I wasn't thinking about what I stole.
I was thinking about who was coming to pick me up.

And when my dad walked in—
it hit me harder than any cop ever could.

He didn't yell.
Didn't scold.
Just looked at me.

I would've given anything for him to scream.
To lose it.
To call me every name in the book.

But he didn't.
And somehow, that was worse.

I was fifteen. Maybe sixteen.
Too young to pay.
Too old to explain.

The cops? A warning.
Like a lost kid at the mall.

No fingerprinting. No lecture.
Just: *She's yours now.*

But if they weren't going to punish me,
my parents would.

My dad took it personally.
I was the Daddy's Girl.
Now I was something else.

A disappointment.

I think he saw it as his failure too.
All that work. All those rules.
And still—I ended up in cuffs.

And my mom?
She didn't yell either.
She looked done.
Tight-lipped. Checked out. Embarrassed.

They didn't even want my sister to know.
Like if they kept it quiet, maybe it wouldn't be real.
Maybe I wouldn't really be *that* kind of daughter.

But I was.
And I had to live with that.

I wish I could say that moment changed me.
That I walked out of the police station brand new.
Ready to turn it all around.

But that's not how it works.
Change sneaks up.
In slow pivots. Quiet truths.

I wasn't fixed.
But I wasn't finished.

the rule follower and the jazz hands

Doctor? Sure—*if scalpels came with jazz hands.*

If my sister was the golden child, I was the glitch.
She had the straight A's, the athlete status, the rulebook on lock.
Perfect on paper.

I pushed limits.
Broke rules.
Stayed in trouble.

I was the creative one.
The unpredictable one.
The one they never fully knew how to handle.

At first, I think they were relieved I liked something.
Dance class? Sure. Great.
At least I was passionate.
But taking it seriously—*career* seriously?
That was a different story.

My sister had no clue what she wanted to do after high school.
She didn't have to decide—when she got a full-ride scholarship to the
Air Force Academy, the path was paved.
No debating. No second-guessing.
She took it.

My parents? Over the moon.
She could do no wrong.

They nodded when I talked about dance.
Smiled politely.
But there was always a pause.
Like they were trying to be supportive—while silently panicking.

At one point, my dad even tried to bribe me:
"Be a doctor and I'll give you a hundred bucks."

A hundred bucks? *Cute.*
I couldn't even clear *Operation* without setting off the buzzer.

But it didn't stop me.
I knew what I was doing.
Or at least—I was willing to figure it out.

Credit where it's due—my mom really showed up.
When I outgrew our small-town studio, she made it work.
Every day after school, she'd pick me up, and we'd drive an hour to Reno.
That became our rhythm.
Two to three classes. Dinner.
Sometimes, another class.

Our go-to spots?
Sizzler.
And Olive Garden—endless breadsticks, bottomless salad, and my
mom sneaking extra mints on the way out.

Meanwhile, the family restaurant was growing.

Dad held things down.
Mom and I had our routine.
School was there.
But dance?
Dance was it.

Not surgeon. Not scholar.
A glittery menace with good turnout and a dream.

Not exactly as planned.
But very on brand.

the comeback and the crash

When you've got nothing left to lose, you become unstoppable.
And when you're doing it for yourself? *That's* when it clicks.

Senior year—one last shot to clean up my act.
The rebellion lingered—quieter now. Sharper.

MTV was everything.
Music videos weren't just entertainment—they were fuel.

Did I think I'd be in them someday? No.
But I had to try.

The difference now?
I wanted it.
I had something to lose.

Cheerleading gave me structure.
Dance gave me fire.
Together, they kept me moving.

I was dancing more than ever.
Ava was my anchor—conventions, choreography, competitions.
Dance wasn't just love anymore.
It was the plan.

No college apps. No fallback.

Just me in my sister's old champagne Honda—
school, cheer, studio, late-night drives to clear my head.

No grades to chase.
No crowds to impress.
Just rhythm. Motion.
And that stubborn hope that doesn't ask permission.

I wasn't waiting.
I was showing up.

One audition. One gig.
One small win at a time.

There was hype around this convention—one of the big ones.
Three days of jazz, ballet, contemporary.
The final day? Scholarship auditions.

A full year in L.A.
Real choreographers. Real training.

Might've been my first real audition.

I remember the room.
Hotel ballroom. Parquet floor. Patterned carpet.
Fluorescent lighting. Stale air.

Hundreds of dancers—stretching, marking, sizing each other up.
At the front: a long table of legends.

We learned a combo. Performed.
They made a cut. Then another.

The room shrank.
The pressure didn't.
Until only a handful were left.

Then the curveball:
"We'd like to see you do a time step."

I blinked.
Wait—what?

Tap wasn't my thing.
Not even close.
Never took a class. Never faked it in the mirror.

My brain scrambled—MTV? No help.
Commercials? Nothing.

The girl to my left? A metronome.
The one to my right? Pure percussion.

Me? I smiled like I might faint.

The teacher leaned in: "Just fake it. You got it."
I nodded. I tried. I really did.

But my feet wouldn't lie—not then, not there.

They wanted me to win. I felt it.

But I gave them nothing.
Only nerves. Silence.
A missed beat that echoed through my whole body.

The moment passed.
The scholarship? Gone.

Winners called. Names announced.
Mine wasn't one of them.

I stood there, smiling. Stunned.
Like *if I stayed frozen long enough, time might rewind.*

No such luck.

I walked off like bones were holding me up.
Made it to the bathroom stall. Collapsed.

The tears weren't loud.
They were tired.
Ashamed to be seen.

It wasn't just disappointment.
It was heartbreak.
The kind that sets up camp behind your ribs and refuses to leave.

I bet everything on this.
And with one time step—I lost the hand.

It felt like the end.
Like I'd auditioned for my future... and got cut.

back to reality

I went back to school like nothing happened.
But I wasn't the same.

I ditched class. Rolled my eyes.
Slipped *back* into that shoulder-shrug version of myself.

What now?
Was the dream dead?

No plan B.
No second act that made sense.

Meanwhile, my dad doubled down on college.
Lab coats. Steady paychecks.
"Be a doctor," he said—waving a hundred bucks like it was magic.
But now he *meant* it.

Make us proud.
Something safe.
Something stable.
Something that wouldn't keep him up at night.

And my friend—
stuck in a dead-end relationship.
No plans. No push.

I dragged her into applying to UNLV with me.
Maybe I was saving her.
Maybe I didn't want to be alone.

So yeah. UNLV.
And what did I choose?
Dance.

Of course.

After all that?
I said *yes* again.

To the thing that let me down.
To the heartbreak and the high.
To the only thing that ever made sense.

Dance.

A waste of money?
Maybe.

What the practical voice said.
What my parents wouldn't say out loud.
What the world shouted every chance it got.

But I didn't care.

Because even wrecked, even doubted—
I *kept* wanting it.
It felt like *mine*, anyway.

And deep down, I was *pissed*.
I had shown up. Worked hard. Given everything.
And the door didn't open.

No callbacks.
Just a quiet that echoed.

But here's the thing:
Even when the world goes quiet, the dream doesn't.

It waits.

Not for applause.
Not for permission.
For me.

I wasn't done.
I wasn't broken.
I was still in it—
bruised, stubborn, and choosing it anyway.

Because no rejection could take away the part that already belonged
to me.

And that part—
wasn't going anywhere.

final thought — no curtain call (yet)

I didn't walk through the door I wanted.
But I didn't walk away either.

I stayed in the hallway—bruised, uncertain, listening for a sign.
Because deep down, I knew:
The door wasn't gone.
Just not open.

And when it does?
I'll be ready.
Not polished.
Not perfect.
But ready.

The dream didn't die when they said no.
It didn't vanish when I froze.
It simply quieted—
waited for me to return.

You don't always get the ovation.
Sometimes the spotlight misses.
Sometimes the moment belongs to someone else.

But if the dream's still alive in your chest—
the curtain rises.

Not done.
Not even close.

✦

off-script

If life's a play, I definitely ad-libbed the hell out of Act II.

the detour

College was never the plan.
Not like it was for other kids—some inevitable next step.

It was filler. A stall.
A holding pattern until something real showed up.

Even then, I knew—once I locked in, I wouldn't let go.
I just hadn't found the right door yet.

And yet, there I was. UNLV.
Dorm life. Meal plans. Syllabus week.
The girl who barely made it out of high school.
Now enrolled in college.

Declared dance major.
Not business. Not nursing. Definitely not pre-med.
Dance.

I could feel the unspoken judgment from every direction:
That's cute—but what's your real major?
You're paying how much to take ballet?
What are you going to do with that?

But I didn't care.
I was there to move. To sweat. To figure it out.

For the first time in a long time, I wasn't cleaning up a mess—only starting something new.

Spoiler: I didn't exactly thrive.
Some classes bordered on parody.
One had us pretending to be trees.

"Sway like wind in the branches," the teacher said, completely serious.
I gave it my best weeping willow.
Four figures for that privilege.

They called it interpretive movement.
I called it bad community theater—with a tuition bill.

College was not the place to actually learn dance.
I lasted a year and a half.
It felt like purgatory in jazz shoes.

Then my dad—bless him—joked he gave up his Mercedes to pay
for my tuition.
Super helpful, Dad.

To stay sane, I took classes off-campus.
Studios with structure. Training that counted.
The only thing grounding me.

Then one day, someone mentioned an audition.
A six-week casino show.
I had no idea what to expect—but I went.

The show was in Laughlin—a border-town casino hub where Nevada, Arizona, and California collide.
Vegas's little cousin—flashy, sweaty, smoky, and just off-brand enough.

The choreographer?
A legit one.
Paula Abdul's Cold Hearted.
Enough said.

I showed up. I danced.
And I booked it.

My first professional dance gig.

cue the peacock

So here I am.
On stage. Like a pro.
Kind of.

My parents were in the audience—ready to see their daughter live out
her big dance dream.
And I step out—

In a bedazzled G-string.
Strapless bra.
Sky-high headpiece.
And a massive feathered back-piece that screamed *Vegas peacock—
extra edition.*

I disappeared behind two lashes, a wing, and a prayer.

Lights: blinding.
Music: thumping like a second heartbeat.
I couldn't feel my face under all that makeup.

I'm sure my dad was mortified.
This? This was the dream?
This was the dance career he gave up his Mercedes for?

I could feel it in his silence: *She is hopeless. Absolutely hopeless.*

And yet... there I was.
On stage. Dancing. Professionally.
G-string, rhinestones, the whole damn spectacle.

Not Broadway.
But booked. Paid. *Mine.*

And for the first time—I felt it.
I'd made it.

JUST A LITTLE BUZZED

magic doors

One of the headliners in the Laughlin show was a magician—older, funny, genuinely kind.
His name was Larry. We clicked right away.

Backstage one night, I told him everything: the dream, the music videos, the hunger for something more.
He listened, then said, "Come out. I'm doing a show at the Magic Castle in Hollywood. I'll show you around."

An invitation.
A shimmer in the static.
A flicker of something else.

Maybe the universe was mending my heart—one feathered, rhinestone-studded moment at a time.

The Magic Castle.
If you've never been—go.
Part haunted mansion, part velvet-draped fever dream.
Magicians everywhere. Card tricks at the bar.
Even the doors feel like they're watching you.

Larry was performing that week.
I said yes.
Stayed with an aunt in Brentwood—a family friend I barely knew.

Asian households are generous with titles. Aunt. Uncle.
It simply means: *you're covered.*

They gave me a room, handed over car keys, and wished me luck with...
whatever this was.

I hit the road—lost half the time, loving every second.
L.A. doesn't come with a manual.
I didn't have a map—just instinct, lip gloss, and a beat-up *Thomas
Guide* I barely knew how to use.

At the Magic Castle, Larry's assistant Julie stepped out in a leopard-
print two-piece under a nurse costume.
She got levitated, sliced in half, disappeared in smoke—then popped
back up like nothing happened.

Campy. Sexy. Ridiculous.
I was obsessed.

Julie and I hit it off fast—and when she couldn't make a gig,
she tapped me in.

Yep, I became the backup nurse-vixen.
One minute in stilettos.
The next—poof. Gone.

Did I belong there? Who knows.
L.A. didn't ask.
It handed me a wand and said: *Try.*

And for once? I didn't need to be found.

Disappearing was never the trick.

Reappearing—on my own terms—that's the real magic.

sidebar: the apple pan

Larry gave me my first taste of classic L.A.—starting with *The Apple Pan*.
L.A. institution. No frills, all flavor.
Red stools. Wax-paper burgers. Pie that *ruins* you in the best way.

Between the sightseeing and smoke machines, I was *still* dancing.
I found a studio—probably while trying to get somewhere else—and
dropped into class.
For the first time in a long time, I felt *good*.
Like I was moving for *me* again.

No grades. No judgment.
Just sweat and music.

After class, the teacher pulled me aside.
"Do you have an agent?"
I blinked. "An agent for what?"
"Dance. You're really good."
My heart thudded.

Next thing I know, he's walking me down to a nearby agency—
introducing me like I was already booked.
"You have to meet this girl."

They were holding auditions the next week.
I showed up. I danced.

They signed me.

Faster than I could process it.
No buildup. No second round.
I was *in*.

Not long after, my agent pulled me aside.
"Casting directors keep butchering your name," she said.
"Think you could shorten it?"

My last name got chopped in childhood—sixteen letters down to three.
Now my *first* name was getting trimmed, too.

Not legally—just optics.
Stage-friendly. Mispronunciation-proof.
A tighter version of *me*.

At that point, my identity was basically an improv set:
Short form. Fast-paced. Made up on the spot.

Two weeks in L.A.
From backup feathers and vanishing vixens...
to a signed dance contract.

Turns out, the magic?
Wasn't only smoke and mirrors.
It was *real*.

exit plan

I went back to Vegas to finish out the semester.
That was the plan—try college, give it a fair shot.
And I did.

But it was obvious—to me, my parents, everyone—that I didn't
belong there.
College wasn't *it*.

Once I know it in my bones, I move.
No waffling. No plan B.
Maybe I got that from my dad.
Even *he* saw it—there was no changing my mind.

I was moving to L.A.
End of story.

But first—I had to deal with a boyfriend.

He'd followed me from Fallon.
Same town, same baggage, new backdrop.
It wasn't love. It was *weight*.
The kind of relationship that doesn't lift you—it presses down.

He didn't just take up space—he swallowed whole pieces of me.
The friendship. The fire. The fun.
I barely recognized myself around him.

And somewhere in the middle of that messy year and a half came a
moment I don't talk about often:

A pregnancy.
An abortion.

Quiet. Private. Life-altering.
It belongs here.

Because that moment cracked something open.
A private decision that became a pivot. A sliding door.
A life I didn't walk through—but *still* carry.

It wasn't easy.
But it was *clear*.
And it was *mine*.

And it taught me more about who I was than any class ever could.

I'd been fading out.
Then, quietly, something clicked back on.

I looked at him and said, straight-up:
"I'm moving to L.A. at the end of the semester. You go wherever you
need to go."

No fight. No drama. Just truth.
I didn't owe him anything else.
That chapter was *closed*.

And with it, I let go of everything that wasn't coming with me—
the weight, the past, the alternate life I could've had.

I chose this one. *Fully*.
And I was ready to live it.

the audition that wasn't

While I was living in Vegas,
I got a call about a national audition for the *Fly Girls* on *In Living Color*.
Rosie Perez was holding open calls in L.A.

This was *huge.*
A dream gig.
The ultimate dance job—style, fire, attitude.
Everything I *lived* for.

My dad insisted on driving me.
Said I shouldn't go alone.
I think part of him wanted to see what I was chasing.

We stayed at a dive motel off Sunset, walking distance to Gower Studios.
That night, he didn't say much—handed me a bottle of water and said,
"Get some rest."

The way he looked at me...
maybe it was the first time he believed I could actually *do* this.

I didn't sleep much.
Wired with adrenaline. Nerves. Hope.

The soundstage was packed.
Hundreds of dancers.

Energy pulsing.
It felt like the *Olympics of cool.*

They lined us up. Looked us over. Made the first cut.

I didn't even get to dance.
Gone. Just like that.

I was *devastated.*
Sat in the car afterward, sobbing.
We'd come all that way, and I didn't even get a chance.

No music. No movement.
A glance.

It was my first real taste of rejection.
And it *stung.*

Not because I didn't book it.
Because I never got to show what I could do.

I kept turning it over:
Is this how it works?
A yes or no—off a single look?
Off... what, exactly?

I didn't have the answer yet.
But the question stayed with me.

And slowly, I became someone
who wasn't afraid to ask *louder.*

final thought: off script

Sometimes the door doesn't open.
Sometimes the dream says *not yet*.
Sometimes you don't even get to dance.

But you show up anyway.

Because even the no teaches you something.
And if you're brave enough to keep going—
you start writing the part they never saw coming.

This time, the script's yours.

No stage directions. No lines to memorize.
Just me—rewiring what it means to arrive.

✦

becoming

No map. Just instinct, grit—and heels that didn't quit.

shedding & shining

When I first moved to L.A., my dad handed me the AMEX and said,
"Don't get a job. Focus on your dream."
Sweet. Supportive. Slightly dangerous.

I got really good at swiping—casually, confidently, like money wasn't real.
Another designer bag I couldn't fit anything in? *Obviously.*
An asymmetrical top I wore once and instantly regretted? *Sure.*

I didn't know the value of money.
Only the thrill of handing over a card that never got declined.

My dad meant well.
It was his version of belief—quiet, generous, slipped across the table
in a silver envelope.

And I took it like a prop.
Swiped my way through L.A., performing like I already belonged.

Then came my first real film gig—*Hot Shots! Part Deux.*
Not glamorous. Not a breakout.
But a real movie. A real set.

Cropped top. Mini skirt.
Camera pointing at me while I fake-danced my heart out.

I played a Raker Girl—budget Laker Girl in a spoof sequel.
Long hair. Tiny outfit. Background choreography.
No lines. No close-up.

But I had a call time. A costume.
A paycheck that said actor.

And somehow—that made it real.
Not the fame. Not the dream.
But the beginning.

A blurry, underpaid, over-caffeinated beginning—
better than anything I'd been promised.

L.A. felt different.
The air, the rhythm, the stakes.

I was chasing auditions. Figuring it out as I went.
Then I booked a job in Paris—a Vietnamese variety show.
Crystal, my best friend, booked it too.
We were green. Deep in our dues-paying phase.

But who cared? *We were going to Paris.*

No rules. No curfew.
Just us—and a production full of equally sleep-deprived performers.

We didn't sleep for days—not from jet lag, but because we didn't want to
miss a second.

We shopped till our feet gave out.

Ate baguettes like it was a sport.
Tried oysters just because.
"If you're gonna do it, do it in Paris," Crystal said. *She was right.*

We wore the Parisian lifestyle like a costume—and it fit.
Tailored to our appetite for more.

We weren't broke.
We were *bougie on a budget.*
Maxing out our per diem like it was Monopoly money.
High on butter with a crust.
High on the freedom to say yes.

Technically, we were there to work.
But it felt like flight.

For the first time, I didn't feel like a dancer in training.
I felt like an artist.
Like I belonged in the world.

That trip flipped a switch.
I came home glowing. Changed.

Then the magic wore off.
Reality thudded back under fluorescent lights.

My agent called. I got an audition.
But the second I walked into that room—number on my chest, sweat in
the air—I wasn't special.
Just another girl with hope stuffed in her shoes and a point to prove.

Music blaring. Heat thick.
I danced like my life depended on it.

Then—nothing.
They made the cut. I didn't.
I stood there, stunned.

It wasn't talent.
I simply looked like everyone else.

Long dark hair. Tan skin. Polished. Predictable.

The universe had dropped a clue.

I wasn't failing.
I was *fading.*
Disappearing into a room I was meant to disrupt.

That night, I talked to my boyfriend.
He said, "Why don't you do something different?"

So I cut my hair.
A little. Then shorter. Then—gone.

A full reset.
Part rebellion. Part reinvention.
Part desperate prayer to be seen.

And suddenly—everything changed.

It was like shedding a skin.
With every inch that fell, I felt lighter. Clearer. *Unmistakable.*
The freedom was addictive.

People noticed.
The bookings followed.

Commercials. Videos. Print.
A bank ad. A McDonald's spot.
A Toyota commercial where I barely blinked.

Didn't matter. *I was visible.*

I don't know if they thought I was fierce or unhinged.
Either way—they remembered me.

I thought buzzing my hair was bold—
then came the *Vanity Fair* shoot in '95.

A Philip Morris ad.
Full scalp. Shiny dome.
Looked like a freshly hatched monk selling cigarettes—
zen but dangerous.

Text projected onto my face—
rebellion dressed as branding.

It was surreal.
And it worked.

Then—
The full-circle moment.

The kind you don't plan.
The kind you recognize by feel.
Eyeliner. Velvet. A charge in the air.

I walked into rehearsal—
and there he was.
The Artist Formerly Known As.
Live. In the flesh.

We were prepping for the American Music Awards.
He didn't walk in. He *arrived.*

Everything I'd ever felt about music, image, power—
he embodied it.
Electric. Regal. Untouchable.

And somehow... *real.*

I stood there, bald head and all, thinking—
I manifested this.

Because maybe I did.

My childhood bedroom was a manifestation board.
Prince. Madonna. Michael.

Symbols of everything I dreamed of becoming.

And now—there he was.
Looking like magic incarnate.
Velvet, eyeliner, the whole thing.

Then came the absurd, glorious world of L.A. dance gigs:

A red bodysuit with a faux-hawk of glued hair—basically a sexy
chicken nugget with choreography.
Hair gelled into cornrows so tight I lost peripheral vision.
A pleather jumpsuit, mid-sandstorm, post-Lasik. Brilliant.
Blue face paint for hours. No explanation. *Just vibes.*
Wig flying off mid-routine. We kept dancing. *Professionals.*
Duct-taped boobs. Clip-in hair.
Heels so high I whispered a prayer with every step—*and stepped anyway.*

And somewhere in all that absurdity—
I found myself.

Ridiculous.
Hilarious.
Raw.
Real.

I was living.
Shedding. Shining.
Becoming.

Not a breakthrough.
A breakout of *my own design.*

And it had only begun.

and then it all hit

It was a blur—bookings, rehearsals, shoots, fittings.
Tour life. Stage life.
Hired gun in heels.

Commercials. Music videos. Stadiums.
Everything I'd imagined—I was doing it.

The world opened fast.
I flew overseas. Met legends. Made lifelong friends.

One week: wandering Amsterdam's Red Light District—weed smoke
curling out of cafés, women in lingerie on display like mannequins
come to life.
A few nights later: tearing through a British award show *like I was on fire.*

Magic. Chaos. All of it.

Hotel living became normal.
The best gigs. The best rooms.
Fans who actually knew my name.

And when the lights hit just right—
pure electricity.

I danced on stages I'd only seen on TV.

Crowds screamed for artists I once worshipped from my bedroom floor.
VMAs. AMAs. Late-night shows.
Dressing rooms with icons, *It girls*, and the *next big thing*.
Backstage rituals like church.
We'd link pinkies before walking out.
No words. Just—*go*.

The thrill was *live*.
Thousands in the crowd.
Collective energy pounding through the floor.

Before every show, I'd touch my buzzed head in the mirror and
whisper,
Let them feel it.

It wasn't about perfection.
It was about *presence. Power.*
Owning the stage with everything I had.

The rush—
a rollercoaster, a sugar hit, a standing ovation.
All at once.

I wasn't just performing. *I was alive.*
Breathing in rhythm. Speaking in sweat.

I was part of something—
a tribe of artists who spoke in 8-counts.
We moved like one body.

Green rooms pulsing with nerves and Red Bull.
Soundchecks so loud we couldn't think.
And when the curtain dropped—
we went.
All in. No holding back.

There were moments.
Music skipping. Timing off. Lights blinding.
Someone slips. Someone saves it.
We keep going.
Backs strong. Breath steady.

Because that's what dancers do—
adjust, recover, make it look effortless.

We hyped each other in sideways glances,
gripped hands before entrances,
nodded low after bows.

We weren't famous.
But *we were there.*
In the eye of the storm.
In the thick of the moment.

That rush—
the bass in your chest,
the lights warming your skin,
the beat syncing with your bones—
it's a kind of high you don't forget.

Everything I'd worked for.
Bled for. Dreamed about.
Everything I'd shed made room for this.

It all collided. Landed.

I was in it.
Fully.
Finally.

no deal

But nothing lasts forever.

Eventually, I realized—
I'd completed the dream on hard mode.
The gigs. The tours. The award shows.
Air miles, paychecks, knee pain—plenty of *how*.
Not a lot of *why*.

The dream hadn't quieted—
I just wasn't listening the same way.

I needed a new kind of chaos.
Something that scared me.
So I started looking sideways—at what else might be possible.
At who else I could be.

Dance had consumed most of my life.
But I started dipping my toes into acting.

Commercials were steady.
A few small roles—enough to taste.
Not enough to call it a break.

Then one day, a call came in—a random TV movie.
I read once. Somehow, I booked it.

I played a woman with power.
Not the quiet kind—the *loud*, dangerous, revenge-driven kind.
A stereotype in silk, pulled from a wildly popular book series
adapted for cable.

I wasn't seasoned, but I held my own.
The director liked me—gave me time, notes, space to grow on camera.

For a second, I thought—*this could be it.*
My pivot. My launch.

Everything on set felt bigger than I was used to.
My own trailer. Actual Blockbuster DVDs dropped off for
downtime—*peak* luxury.
Special meals. People checking on me like I was the star.

I remember thinking—*Wait... am I the lead and no one told me?*

The male lead and I hit it off—friendly, easy, light.
We shared scenes. Laughed between takes.
Apparently, the lead actress noticed. Clocked it. *Hard.*
And suddenly, the vibe shifted.

My trailer got moved.
From the heart of the set... to exile at the edge of the lot.

At first, I thought it was *her*—jealousy, maybe.
But something didn't sit right.

Then came the lunch.
Random restaurant. A woman at the next table—talking about
the book series.
About the director.
Something clicked. Slowly, then all at once.

It wasn't *her*.
It was *him*.
The stories. The subtext I hadn't wanted to see.

I was dumbfounded.

After that, he called. Said people might reach out. Told me to be
honest.
I remember saying, "I have nothing to tell. Nothing happened."

But the fact that he reached out—*before* they did?
That was plenty.

Hollywood, for all its shine, has a dark side.
This was pre-Weinstein.
Pre-headlines. Pre-exposés.
Before the wave of voices finally broke through.
Back then, it was simply *how it worked*.

I got offers. The kind with strings.
Private dinners. Backdoor casting conversations.
Promises wrapped in unspoken expectations.

I knew the shortcut.
I saw the path.

I didn't take it.
One night in Düsseldorf, I woke up mid-panic.
No logic—only dread.
Convinced something had happened to my boyfriend.

Threw on a hoodie. Barefoot. Tear-streaked.
Ran to the lobby payphone—because international cell service
wasn't a thing—and finally got him on the line.

He'd gotten into an accident.
He was okay.
But I was unraveling.

I stood there, breathing hard—hoodie clinging to my back.
Ding. The elevator.
I stepped in, breath shaky, mind spinning.
As the doors began to close, a man slipped in.
The energy flipped.
Fast. Entitled. Invasive.
Like I was *there for him.*

The second those doors opened, I bolted.
He shouted after me down the hallway.

I was shaking. Furious.

I called the front desk. Told them what happened.
They brushed it off like I'd complained about slow room service.

So I laced up my Timbs like I was about to start a riot and stormed
back downstairs.

There he was. Sitting at the bar. Calm as ever.
I lost it. Caused a scene.
Cursed him out in a blur of English, adrenaline, and
don't-fuck-with-me rage.

He saw me coming and panicked—made for the door.
And I shouted after him, loud enough for the whole damn lobby:

"Oh wait, I thought you wanted some? I'm right here."

He ran.
And I chased him—out of the hotel. Into the night.

Two people from my crew were nearby—either backing me up or
trying to calm me down, I honestly don't remember.
What I do remember?
Boots on pavement. My rage in my throat.
And not a single hotel employee stepping in.

Later, someone told me that hotel was known for sex workers in the
lobby—women waiting to be picked up.
And for a second, I wondered—*Did he think I was one?*

Not that it would've made it okay.
But it reminded me:
Even mid-tour, mid-dream—
You're *someone else's* fantasy.
Someone else's target.

And sometimes?
You're also the girl in boots, chasing him into the street.

Even some friends made offers.
The kind that left me unsure—flattered? Offended? Flat-out *tired*.
Maybe they thought their honesty made it okay.
Maybe I was naive to think they ever saw me as more than access.

I thought I had a lot of male friends.
Turned out—I didn't.

And sure—maybe I could've gotten further. Faster.
More posters. More carpets. A household name.

But I chose sleep.
I chose peace.
I chose *knowing* I could look in the mirror and like who looked back.

That's its own kind of fame.
Not loud. Not trending.
But solid. *Mine.*

And that movie?
It was a sign.
Also—a little painful.

I cringed when I watched it.
I was terrible. Like, so bad.

But hey—*why not immortalize your worst performance on film forever?*

I was double-dipping.
One foot in the dance world.
One foot reaching for... *something.*

I didn't know it yet,
but the final gig was around the corner.

And *it had plans for me.*

the final gig

I thought I was coasting toward the end.
But the industry had other plans.
One last tour. One final test.

This time, the lesson hit different.

She was young.
Undeniably talented. Freshly famous.
Still figuring out who she was.

Some days, I was her big sister. Her hype woman. Her safe place.
Other days, I was *the threat.*

I didn't play the game.
Wasn't a yes-girl. Never have been.
What I brought to the table was *truth.*
She saw that. Felt it.
And maybe—*resented it.*

I lifted her up. Praised her talent.
But eventually, it wasn't enough.

I was pulling too much attention.
Too seen. Too admired.
Too... *me.*

The guys liked me.
The crowd noticed me.
And suddenly, that became a problem.

She never said it out loud.
But the volume was unmistakable.

One day, we were in the Midwest.
Morning radio interview—she said something off.
By that afternoon, we were kicked out of our hotel.

Not *moved*.
Kicked out.

Management scrambled.
Dancers dragged suitcases into the parking lot.
No real explanation.

We did the show anyway.
Of course we did.

But the crowd?
They weren't having it.

Mid-set, a tomato flew.
An *actual tomato*.

We weren't just losing the audience.
We were losing *the illusion*.

It wasn't the tomato.
It was a message. A metaphor.
Ego. Entitlement.
The kind of spotlight that burns hotter than it shines.

Eventually, I asked her what was going on.
She didn't dodge.

She told me she admired me.
Said I was fearless. That people liked me for being *me*.
And that's what she wanted.

It hit me in the softest, strangest place.
I wasn't trying to be anything.
I was simply doing my job.

But in this industry?
Being yourself is often the biggest threat in the room.

So I started playing small.
Not because I wanted to.
Because I had to.

To survive the day.

It felt like punishment—
for *not* dimming fast enough.

And I tried.
God, I tried.

But once you've lived in your light,
you can't *unknow* it.
You can't *unlove* it.
You can't *unsee* it.

And you sure as hell can't pretend
you were never meant to shine.

The truth?
I didn't walk away.
I got fired.

Not for messing up—
for taking up too much space.

Too visible.
Too confident.
Too unwilling to play small.

And with that—
everyone turned.

Dancers I'd shared buses, green rooms, takeout, and late-night tears
with—gone. Silent.

Avoiding me like I was contagious.

They had to survive too.
I get it.

They couldn't risk being seen with me.
I was radioactive—
a threat to their paychecks.

I don't blame them.
But I won't forget it.

Maybe I saw it coming.
But that didn't soften the blow.

This industry, it'll split you in two.
Build you up. Crown you—
then strip you bare to see what's left.

It can eat your worth.

It's beautiful.
And it's brutal.

But it doesn't get to define you.

Because *I already knew who I was.*
And if that chapter had to end
for the next one to begin?
So be it.

I walked out with my integrity intact.
And *that was enough.*

The last curtain dropped.
The noise fell away.

And in the quiet that followed,
I knew—
I was done.

what stayed was mine

When I look back at that version of me—the girl with the shaved head,
standing in the spotlight, dancing her heart out while *quietly falling
apart*—I don't feel shame.
I feel *compassion*.

She was doing her best in a world that didn't know what to do with
girls like her.
She loved hard. Worked harder.
Showed up—cold rooms, sharp stares, her name whispered like a warning.
She was breaking in places no one could see—
and *still*, she danced.

And when the music stopped?
She kept moving anyway.

That chapter didn't end the way I imagined.
But maybe it ended *exactly* how it needed to.

Because when the lights faded and the tour was over, something else
began—
a deeper truth. A fuller self. A *new voice*.

And that girl? She didn't disappear.
She *evolved*.

No matter what anyone tried to take—her spotlight, her place,
her power—
what stayed was *hers*.
The knowing. The grit. The light.

And this?
This was only the beginning.

I take class now.
Not to book a job or prove anything.
I circled back, years later—
and this time, it's *different*.

No competition. No comparisons.
No mirror marathons of critique.

Moving with intention.
Feeling without judgement.
Reclaiming what was always mine.

Sometimes I see old friends in class—people I danced with years ago.
We don't always say much, but we share that quiet nod: *we're here.*

Old friends—some now teachers.
Familiar rooms. Familiar faces.
It feels like rehearsal again—softer. Different.

We stretch for real now.
We hydrate because we have to.
We cheer for each other like it's still 1998—just with better insurance.

The nostalgia hits—but with *new eyes*.
We joke that we can never stop dancing—
not for the poetry or the soft-light, turmeric-latte
"movement is medicine" posts—
but because if we stop,
it might take *three years and a few cortisone shots*
to get the groove back.

It's still in there.
Beneath the Advil and adult responsibilities.
Deep in the muscle memory.

And honestly?
It feels *damn* good.

Same floor. More creaks. More grit.
Still worth every step.

✦

To the girl in the studio mirror—

You don't know it yet,
but all that weirdness, all that unapologetic too-much-ness,
all those loud outfits and quiet doubts?

They're not mistakes.
They're *magic*.

One day, you'll realize you weren't meant to be liked by everyone.
You were meant to be *seen*.

To move the room simply by being in it.
One day, you'll walk into a studio—older, softer, stronger—
and see yourself in someone else.
And you'll want to tell her:

You're already *enough*.
Always have been.
Still magic. Keep going.

✦

I'm not chasing the spotlight anymore.
But I know how to *flip the switch*.
On myself. On others.
On the whole damn room if I have to.

No dimming. No apologies.
Just light—*aimed with precision*.

Call it a gift.
Call it payback.
Call it *grown*.

The light never left.
It just took a detour—through velvet stages, casting rooms,
and a *Vanity Fair* ad where I looked like a *freshly hatched monk pushing
luxury cigarettes*.

And then—the ripple reached me back.

A few years after I'd stepped away, I was having a drink with an old

friend when a sweet Japanese girl approached me.
"I used to watch you on MTV back home and tried to dance like you,"
she said. "Thank you. You inspired me."

That moment?
Proof that it all mattered.
Proof that someone saw me—
and *believed they could be next.*

Legacy doesn't always arrive with applause.
Sometimes it walks up quietly—
bows—
and says: *thank you.*

It's not always loud.
But it *echoes.*
In mirrors. In memory. In movement.
In *whoever dares to go next.*

✦

the fire and the ashes

She saw ashes.
I saw a blueprint.

pedestals are lonely places

The last tour asked me to shrink, dim, fit a mold.
But the truth is—I'd already been doing that to myself.

I'd climbed a pedestal without even realizing—
thought it would keep me safe. *Seen. Loved.*

But pedestals?
They're not built to hold anyone.

I used to hand them out like party favors—*golden, loyal, untouchable.*
Until the betrayal hit harder than expected.
And I was left wondering—*how did I not see it?*

That's the danger: pedestals hide the fractures.
And while I was busy propping others up, I stayed on mine.
Painted it gold. Kept it spotless.
Didn't see the cracks—*until it collapsed.*

What if they saw me—and didn't like it?
Acting let me wear someone else's skin.
Speak their words. Feel their pain.
It was vulnerability with a built-in escape hatch.

Eventually, therapy gave it a name: *perfectionism.*
The kind that starts in childhood and clings like static.

The kind you cry about in your car after deep sessions.
The kind that whispers even after years of healing.
Because deep down, I wasn't performing to deceive—
I was *trying to belong.*

But eventually, the mask slipped.
And the applause felt hollow.

The people I'd placed so carefully on pedestals?
They showed their sharp edges.

That one glittery friend?
Her digs got louder.
Loyalty turned conditional.
Trust evaporated.

And I didn't want to believe it—because if I admitted it,
I had to admit *I saw it coming.*

The pedestal I built for myself? Just as fragile.
Every flaw felt fatal. Every misstep, a reason I didn't deserve love.
I didn't know how to be loved *without earning it.*

But pedestals don't protect you—they isolate you.
They keep you above real connection.
Above mess.
Above healing.

I keep learning to let people be people—
not idols. Not villains. Not projects.

And I'm learning to just be a person, too.

No spotlight. No script.
Here—*cracked, clear-eyed, and real.*

Wild, how long you can live holding your breath,
waiting for someone else to say it's okay to exhale.
But that voice?
It doesn't stick unless it comes from *inside.*

Some days, they sneak back in—old habits, old scripts.
To over-give. Over-explain. Shrink.
Whatever feels safer.

And then I pause.
Come back to my breath. My body.
To the part of me that knows:

I don't have to earn love by disappearing.

The real work isn't about being better.
It's about *being braver.*

Letting yourself be seen—for the highlight reel
and the scared little kid who wants
to know she's allowed to stay.
Even if she messes up.
Especially then.

And once I let myself be seen—*really* seen—
I couldn't unsee everything else.

The quiet politics.
The fake nice.
The way women like me get labeled *difficult* for having boundaries.

I saw the old rules—
smile, shrink, stay shiny, behave.

Hard pass.

I was done performing.
Done handing out passes to people who hadn't earned them.
Done mistaking silence for peace.

It wasn't dramatic.
It was *necessary*.

I stopped explaining.
Stopped over-apologizing.
Stopped twisting myself into something more palatable.

Turns out, *freedom* looks a lot like *not giving a damn*—
and *meaning it*.

the libra assignment

Justice has always mattered to me.
Maybe it's the *Libra* in me—October 9th, thank you very much.
Same birthday as a few saints. Also John Lennon.
And yes... a serial killer too—*just to keep it balanced.*

Fairness wasn't a concept.
It was *physical.*

I could *feel* it—deep in my chest—when something was off.
When someone got mistreated.
When a room turned cold toward the wrong person.
When a teacher played favorites.
When someone took credit for work they didn't do.

I couldn't ignore it.
I always spoke up—even when it cost me.

Brave? *Sure.*
Exhausting? *Every time.*

Sometimes the one who speaks up is the one who gets left out.
But silence never sat right.

I wasn't trying to be a hero—
I wanted things to be right.

I've learned to pick my battles better now.
Not everything needs a crusade.
Just most things.
But that justice chip?
Still *fully* installed.

Even with my compass locked in, the world kept spinning sideways—
unfair, impossible to fix.

I kept showing up.
Speaking out.
Trying to make sense of it all—
until the chaos swallowed any sense I had left.

cracks in the system

Eventually, I got dissatisfied—with myself, with the world.
Everything felt like a contradiction.
Nothing made sense.

So I did what I always do when things feel broken—
I *tried to fix it.*
Fix me. Fix them. Fix *everything.*

But where do you start when you don't even know what's broken?
Where else do you go when you're looking for answers?
Church, obviously.

I showed up like the perfect little student—
notebook packed. Lip gloss on. *Spirit... open-ish.*

Then the pastor said to give up our luxuries—
clothes, jewelry, the unnecessary things.

Excuse me?

I looked down at my outfit.
Chosen with care. Layered. Mood-matching.

This wasn't luxury.
This was *survival.*

I wanted to be moved. I really did.
But not at the expense of my *boots*.

And just like that—
Sunday service was over.

I realized I could talk to God *anywhere*. *Anytime*.
No permission required. No middleman needed.

So I pivoted.
Tried new things. Explored other paths.

If God wasn't in the church,
maybe He was in the *high*.
In the *surrender*.
In the *drop*.

And maybe He was.
Or maybe I needed to fall apart
before I could put myself back together.

But the search didn't stop—it got deeper.
Riskier.
Stranger.
Closer to home.

I wasn't just questioning the world anymore.
I was starting to question *myself*.

Not in a doubting way—
in a *what else is in there?* kind of way.

ecstasy and the quiet awakening

Yeah—drugs.
Ecstasy was having a moment back then.
And quietly... so was I.

I wasn't chasing the party.
I was chasing stillness.
Connection.
A break from the static.

I wasn't trying to escape.
I was trying to return—
to a part of myself I hadn't met yet.

At first, it felt like therapy.
Everything softened.
Walls lowered.
The noise in my head finally quieted down.

It felt like love.
Like truth.
Like finally hearing myself.

But like most things that feel too good—
I went too far.

One night, I overdid it.
No idea how many I took.
But I remember my legs giving out.
Just—gone.

I slid to the floor.
Fully alert.
Trapped in a body that wouldn't move.

Lights. Sounds. Edges blurring.
Something was wrong.

Then—I felt it.
A seizure. Slow. Creeping.
Not dramatic. But undeniable.
A quiet hijacking of my nervous system.

And somehow—
I stayed present.

Heard everything. Saw everything.
I couldn't respond.

But deep inside, a voice.
Not frantic. Not afraid. Just... steady.

You're okay. Stay here. Breathe.

I repeated it like a mantra I didn't know I had.

Held my own hand. In a body that wouldn't move.
Refused to disappear.

It was terrifying.
But also—oddly empowering.

Even when everything was shutting down,
some part of me stayed.
Present. Aware. Refusing to go dark.

That voice?
That was me, too.
Not wise. Not glamorous. Not safe.
But mine.

It unlocked something in me.

It showed me that even when I feel powerless,
there's a core in me that knows how to come back.

That night scared me.
But it reminded me:

I've always known what to do.

And sometimes, you have to fall that far—
to hear yourself clearly.

healing in all the places

Therapy. Again.

One therapist told me he couldn't help me—said I was too nice,
that people probably steamrolled me my whole life.

Thanks, doc. Super enlightening.

So I kept going.
Psychics. Healers. Mystics.
Ayahuasca *(yes, that trip)*.
Self-help books. Journaling. Breathwork.
Crying in parked cars, of course.

Meditation. Regression. Reframing.

I wasn't trying to *heal*—
I was trying to *understand.*
Trying to name the weight. *Lift the fog.*

And honestly?
I don't regret the detour.

Pills, plants, prayers—
they didn't fix me.

But they brought me *closer to myself.*

I wasn't chasing *answers.*
I was chasing *reminders.*

Something to tell me I wasn't broken.
That maybe
I already knew what I needed to know.

For a long time, I kept looking outside myself.
Searching the sky for signs.
Waiting for clarity—
for someone to tell me what to do. Who to be. Where to go.

But eventually, I realized:
The map wasn't out there.
It was in me.
It always had been.

All the mystics, medicine, and mantras didn't give me anything new.
They helped me remember:
the compass was internal.

The ache and the pull I kept feeling weren't distractions—
they were directions.

The truth doesn't always arrive with flashing lights.
Sometimes it just... *hums.*

And even when you finally *hear it,*
living it is something else entirely.

Some patterns are *sticky*.

Especially the ones that masquerade as *love*.

the cost of giving

Meanwhile, another layer of confusion was brewing:
Being spoiled came with guilt.

I could feel the jealousy. The tension.
The unspoken *Why you?*
So I gave more than I got—*on purpose.*

If I bought shoes, I bought a pair for them, too.
If I had more, I gave more—especially in love.
I paid for everything. Took care of them.

That's how Dad showed love—through gifts.
So I learned to love that way too.

Give more. Do more. Be more.
Disappear more.

But it left me wondering:
Were they here for me... or for what I could give them?

That question didn't stay in relationships.
It crept into everything—friendships, work, even art.

It twisted my reasons for giving.
And made me more guarded than I realized.

One birthday, I bought a friend a shirt.
Picked it out thoughtfully. Wrapped it with care.
I was excited to give it to her.

She opened it in front of a crowd, held it up, and said,
"I'll never wear this. You can return it."

Not cruel, exactly.
Just... *not kind.*

To this day, I catch myself wondering—
Was she blunt?
Trying to prove something?
Expecting more?

It landed soft.
But it bruised deep.

I laughed it off,
but it stuck. *And it stayed.*

That moment made me flinch.
And I never gave the same way again.

Because when generosity gets dismissed like that—
it messes with your wiring.

It makes you question your instincts.
Your thoughtfulness.
Your worth.

Learning to receive without guilt—
and to give without losing myself—
took time.

But it started with that one uncomfortable truth:
Some people loved the giving more than the giver.

Some truths don't land all at once.
They simmer—*until they burn.*

And when it did, what was left surprised me.

I think that's how the best transformations happen.
You live. You lose. You learn.

And then?
You burn the pedestal down.

And with the ashes—
you build something true.
Something rooted.
Something that finally feels like home.

✦

knit, purl, pivot

Unraveling isn't failure.
It's foreshadowing.

when the music stopped

Post-dance, I fell into a quiet kind of darkness—the kind where silence feels safer than sound.

I couldn't listen to music. Couldn't watch music videos.
It hurt too much.
My body wanted to move, but my heart couldn't bear it.
Even a beat over the speakers at Target felt like betrayal—
like hearing from an ex who ghosted you.
One second you're fine.
The next, you're crying in front of the discounted paper towels.

I had to cut it all out—like a breakup that went too deep.
The grief sat heavy. Quiet. Like a phantom limb.
But worse—because no one could see the missing limb.

Music had always defined me.
And now, without it, I was floating. No anchor.

I quit cold turkey.
No farewell tour. No closure. Just silence—and the question I couldn't answer:
Who am I now?

And like most overachievers in grief, I threw myself into the next thing: acting.

Commercials were steady. But I wanted more—
more than cameos. More than smiling while someone else led the story.
I wanted depth. Challenge. Disappearance.
To become someone else—because being myself felt too raw.

So I became a student again. Hours in class. Chasing craft like a lifeline.
If I couldn't dance it out, I would speak it. Cry it. Breathe it.

But the roles for Asian women? Same four options:
Hooker, doctor, cop, or ninja in a bikini with a PhD.

The roles were thin. The writing thinner. And the notes?
Usually some version of: *Can you make her more exotic?*
Or: *Try that again, but... mysterious?*

Some rooms felt like traps.
Smiles on entry. Gut punch by callback.

"You're Asian, but not Asian enough," one casting director said,
squinting like I might morph on command.
Another asked, "What kind of Asian are you?"—like they were
ordering takeout.
One thought I was Black.
Another handed me a long black wig and said, "Let's see if it
helps you read... right."

Character breakdowns were always a riot:
*mysterious but grounded. sexy but soft. accent optional. cry on cue—but
quietly, and hot. authenticity negotiable.*

To be fair, not all casting directors were like that.
Some were generous. Curious. Grounded in actual storytelling.
But the bad ones? Unforgettable.

I didn't exactly make it easy.
My headshot changed weekly. My vibe? Day-dependent.
One day: backup dancer. The next: boutique hedge fund HR.
They didn't know what to do with me.
Neither did I.

I missed dance.
Dance didn't lie.
Your body showed up—or it didn't.
The audience felt you—or they didn't.
No scripts. No typecasting. Just movement and truth.

Acting had truth, too—but it was buried.
Buried under tone, type, approval-seeking.

Even so, I kept showing up—for myself, for the work.
And sometimes, it mattered. I booked things. Small things. Glimmers
of *maybe.*

But nothing stuck quite the same. Nothing felt like dance.
It wasn't just a job. It was the love. The language.
The thing that lit me up from the inside out.

Without it, I felt like a translation of myself—
almost the same, but not quite.

Eventually, I stopped chasing. Not out of defeat.

Out of clarity.
Because I didn't need to become someone else to feel worthy.
I didn't need to get the part to have a part.
I needed a new way to move.

And that's where the next spark came in—unexpected. Handmade.

It wasn't dance.
But it held rhythm. Repetition. Precision.
Even a little... meditation.

It was yarn.
And the slow, strange magic of starting something from nothing.

✦

But before the yarn, there was this moment:

Acting class could be electric—when the teacher was the real deal.
Some were. You could feel it.
But others were just playing the part. *Performing wisdom instead of teaching it.*

Some days, the air in class felt thick.
Too many actors. Not enough truth.
Everyone performing—even when no one was watching.

The teacher ran it like a mind game: praise, then gut-punch.
"You're magnetic," followed by, "You don't live in your body."
Backhanded notes dressed up as breakthroughs.

People nodded like it was gospel.
I sat there thinking—*Seriously?*
This wasn't truth. It was a power trip.

And I called bullshit.

After class, I waited.
Everyone filed out, high on confusion and praise.
I walked up to him.
"Can I ask something?"

He smiled, like I was about to ask for a book rec.

"That scene earlier... you said it was great. Alive. Connected. Then two minutes later, you said it lacked truth. That they weren't in their bodies."

He didn't respond.

"I'm not trying to challenge you," I said. "But we're here to grow, right? When feedback's vague or contradictory, it doesn't help. It spins people out.
If something's not working—say so. But don't play games. Just be real."

The energy snapped.

I almost didn't say it.
I'd spent years staying quiet to keep the peace.

He squinted. Tilted his head.
"You seem to have a chip on your shoulder," he said.
"Maybe try connecting with the class. Make some friends."

I blinked.

"I didn't pay to make friends," I said. "I paid to get better."

He just nodded. Dismissively.
I walked out.

Maybe I was the only one who saw it.
Or the only one who said it out loud—even quietly, even alone.

Because here's what I learned:
Silence doesn't protect you. It swallows you.

So I stopped letting things slide.

I didn't show up for approval.
I showed up for the work.

The silence didn't stay empty.
It became yarn. Movement.
A different kind of choreography.

knitting obsession becomes a spark

I've never been great at stillness.
Even when my body stopped, my brain kept running—loops, lists, ideas, existential spirals.
So when the gigs slowed and the dance chapter ended, I didn't know what to do with the space.

I filled it with yarn.

It started on set. Between takes, I'd pull out my knitting.
It was having a moment—a quiet little trend bubbling up among creatives.
Most people started with scarves.
I went full throttle: a cardigan. Cables. Buttons. *The whole cozy saga.*
Something to keep my hands busy and my mind quiet.

The first one was a mess—one sleeve longer than the other, neckline off, buttons spaced like I'd eyeballed them in the dark.
But it had heart. Imperfect. A little weird.
Weird in the best way—the kind that makes people smile.

Then a friend wore it out—and came back glowing.
Said a boutique wanted to know if I could make more.
I laughed. It had taken me a month.
Obsessive knitting, every spare second.
I would've had to charge *West Hollywood rent* to break even.

And yet... the idea stuck.

So I made another.

I remember knitting for hours and only ending up with half a sleeve.
A friend looked at me and said, "Girl, you're too young to be knitting
like this. Try kids. They're smaller."
She had a point.
So I did.

Toddler sweaters. Mini sleeves. Tiny collars.
And you know what?
They were good.
Like—*legit* good.

But this was L.A.—land of eternal sunshine.
Sweaters weren't exactly flying off shelves.
And they definitely didn't scream scalable.

So I pivoted: casual streetwear. Tees. Hoodies. Play-all-day pieces.
Simple. Wearable. Smart.

And just like that—the next chapter found me.

The yarn gave me something to do with my hands.
Then it gave me something to build.
Then it gave me an idea I couldn't ignore.

I didn't go looking for a fashion brand.
I just wanted to make something.
Something beautiful.

Something that felt like mine.

And suddenly—there it was.
A path I hadn't expected.
But it made perfect, weird, beautiful sense.
Like something I'd been stitching toward all along.

There's a moment right before the idea lands.
Not flashy. Not loud. Just... *aligned.*
Like every detour, every quiet yes, was leading here.

Not back to the stage.
But to center.
To craft.
To me.

what I carried forward

I don't circle back the same way.
Not once I've said goodbye to the version that no longer fits.
Not with people. Not with jobs. Not with dance.

When I walk away, it's because something gave way.
And once it does, I don't glue it back.
I move forward.

Dance was everything once—*my oxygen, my identity.*
Leaving it felt like losing a limb.
But I didn't bleed out.
I stopped chasing it to survive.

I didn't abandon it.
I just stopped charging it rent.
Kept the joy. The magic.
Let it live in my body—*without a paycheck attached.*

Then fashion came in—new, unexpected, a little wild.
Like falling in love again.

But this time, I wasn't just performing.
I was building.

And I had to be all in—present, scrappy, committed.
I nurtured it like a seed. Showed up every day—
even when I had no clue what I was doing.

Because I believed in it—*fully*.
This wasn't clothing.
It was *purpose*.
It was a voice that could reach further than dance ever could—
to kids across the globe.
To places I'd never even set foot.

Through this brand, I found new ways to give.
Built bathrooms in villages that had none.
Sent money where it mattered.
Sent clothes to orphanages. Helped schools that still believed in art.
Backed communities where creativity was on life support.

It wasn't performative.
It was personal.

Because I remembered what it felt like to want more—
and not know how to ask for it.

I wasn't dressing kids.
I was speaking to them.
To the bold. The quiet.
The weirdos. The dreamers. The soft rebels.

And maybe, in some small way, I was speaking to *her*—
the little girl version of me.
The one who didn't always fit.

The one who needed something that said: *You belong.*

That became the reason.
That became the art.

My next teachers didn't stand at the front of a class.
They stood behind sewing machines.
Espresso counters.
Boardrooms. Back offices.

And they taught me every bit as much—
about grit, vision, generosity, and getting shit done.
No spotlight. No applause.
Impact.

from fabric to family

I don't remember the exact moment it began.
One day I was on my hands and knees, digging through a bin of
buttons in a downtown L.A. factory.
I walked showrooms. Roamed the fashion district.
Learned by doing.

No fashion degree. No formal training.
And maybe that was the gift.
I didn't know the rules—so I broke them.

It was instinct. Trial. Error. Curiosity. Repeat.

Ignorance wasn't bliss.
It was freedom.

Stick-figure sketches turned into patterns.
Patterns turned into samples.
Zippers where they didn't belong.
Pockets that made no sense—*until they suddenly did.*

Every piece had its own kind of poetry.

I was buying fabric from Switzerland.
Precise. Beautiful.
Also? *Ridiculous.*

I had no business sourcing $100-a-yard textiles for toddler clothes.
But I didn't care.
I was chasing a feeling—
a gut pull I couldn't explain but couldn't ignore.

People doubted me. Even friends.
They smiled politely, nodded supportively—
but I could feel it: *Is this a phase?*
It wasn't.

I had jumped into something that made no logical sense—
and everything inside me said: *Go.*
So I did. *Headfirst. All heart. Zero backup plan.*

And when I needed them, the right teachers showed up.
Helpers of all kinds.
Guiding. Correcting. Encouraging.
Divine timing dressed as factory wisdom.

I spent a lot of afternoons at Mauro's Cafe at Fred Segal—
long lunches that bled into wine-soaked evenings.

The owners became my Italian family.
It wasn't just a restaurant.
It was iconic L.A.—a scene, a cultural crossroads,
where stylists, celebrities, and dreamers collided over pasta and espresso.

Fred Segal on Melrose is gone now.
Closed, like so many L.A. staples.
But back then? *It was magic.*
Like something out of a scene I forgot I was writing.

At the time, I was repping a boutique wine brand—short-lived, but
pivotal.
The owner had one dream account: Mauro's Café.
Everyone said it was impossible.
Too high-profile. Too loyal to longtime vendors.

I walked in, struck up a conversation—
and somehow, instant friendship.
It wasn't a pitch. It wasn't forced.
It clicked.

They said *yes* on the spot.

That account became more than a checkbox.
It became a doorway.
A spark.
A beginning I didn't see coming.

What started as a wine meeting turned into a creative kinship.
I wasn't there to hustle—I was there to connect.
And somehow, they let me in.

Through them, I met people. *Real* ones.
Collaborators. Friends.
Unexpected doors opened without knocking.

I didn't go to build a business.
I went to be fed.
Spiritually. Creatively.

But it all fed the business, too.

Word got out.
People started showing up—
random, brilliant creatives who wanted in.
Even when I couldn't pay them, they stayed.
Because they felt it, too—
that *this* was something.

Monika, a retail fairy godmother, floated in from the children's
department—
calm, quietly brilliant, overqualified.
She broke down the system like a human cheat sheet.
We became friends.

Sean, a true artist.
Tuned into my vision like he could read my mind.

The reps came next.
So did the interns—quirky, wide-eyed, ready to dive in wherever
needed.

I built a brand.
Named it.
One lead opened the next.
Each *yes* lit the path to another.

I stayed humble.
Curious.
Willing.

And then one day, I looked up—
and there it was: a full collection.

But the real shift came quietly.

I was sitting in acting class—quiet, raw, trying to heal—
when the guy next to me, Ted, struck up a conversation.
Somehow, the clothing line came up.
He listened. *Really* listened.

Then he said:
"That's a great idea. What would it take to start?"

I told him.

And he cut me a check.

Right there.
A total stranger.
An angel in street clothes.
A divine nudge.
The first real yes.

When you're ready, the universe sends people.
And I was ready.
And Ted? Total brother-from-another-mother energy.
Kind. Encouraging. Real.
One of the first people who gave without asking for anything back.

no one told me I couldn't

I had the collection.
Now it was time to sell.
Another mountain. *No map.*

I didn't know fashion seasons had deadlines—
or that buyers placed orders months in advance.
So I did what I always do—
picked up the phone.

West Coast reps. East Coast reps.

"The season's closed."
"Call us next year."
"Nothing's moving."

So I *moved.*

I booked a flight to New York with my samples,
a rolling rack, a laptop, and a whole lot of fire.
Rented a car.
Hit the road—cold-calling every kids' boutique I could find.
Research done. List made. *Doors knocked.*

I'd hype myself up in the car,
then walk in like I belonged—
rolling rack first, story second.

And it worked.
One store after another said yes.
Some instantly. Others, surprised:
"Wait... this is actually good."
It was.

Most days, it felt less like selling clothes
and more like doing stand-up in a borrowed parking lot.
No script. No stage crew.
Me, a trunk full of hope, a rack of dreams,
and an audience that didn't know they'd bought tickets.

Half hustle, half miracle.
Full send—step right up, folks.

So I did it again.
Midwest. West Coast.

Thirty-four stores.
No rep. No showroom. No trade show.

Then I called those reps back:
Didn't you say no one was buying this season?

They couldn't deny me.

Word started to spread—boutique buzz, coast to coast.
A few buyers took notice.
And suddenly, the girl with no fashion degree, no showroom, no rules—
was everywhere.

Not because I knew what I was doing.
But because I did it anyway.

all in, hands on

Production mattered. *Made in USA mattered.*
I found a factory and learned everything I could—pattern-making, grading, cutting, sewing.
It wasn't glamorous. I didn't care.

I wore every hat: designer, sales rep, delivery girl.
Picked up bolts of fabric from the dye house, tossed them into my Prius, hauled them across the city, dropped them off—then did it all again.

Augustine, the main sewer, spoke English. The rest were Spanish-speaking—kind, quiet, curious.
They watched me come and go, week after week, until one day he asked, "Who's the owner?"

"I am."

He blinked. "Owners don't come here. They don't carry bags. They don't talk to us."

But I did. "Hi. Thank you. See you next time."
Not to prove anything—*because I didn't know any other way to be.*

They became my people. *My factory family.*
I brought donuts. Hung out. Learned names. Listened.

They taught me what no syllabus could:
How to feel fabric with your palm and *know what it wants to become.*
How to fix a jam mid-run without flinching.
How to move with precision, not panic.

Even the basics had rhythm—folding, packing, labeling.
Not just to ship, but *to honor the work.*

Ray, the cutter, gave me 5:30 AM lessons—step by step.
Karate Kid: Factory Edition.
If I cut corners, he made me start over.
I wasn't making clothes.
I was earning my place.

I picked up some Spanish—the real kind. (*Shoutout to four years of high school Spanish that taught me absolutely nothing.*)
Learned fast. Swore faster. Understood just enough to catch when I was being roasted.

The factory? Loud. Dusty. Chaotic.
But to me? *It felt like a mixtape.*
Rough. Honest. Unexpected.
A mashup of hustle, noise, and rhythm—stitched together by something sacred I didn't have words for yet.

Because this wasn't a business.
It was mine. *All in. All heart.*

I used to think learning looked like classrooms and whiteboards.
Turns out, mine were *threading needles at sunrise.*

✦

Back in my design days, I had this thing—everything had to be truly unique.
Not kind-of different.
Not *add a patch and call it a day* different.
I mean handcrafted. Borderline unreasonable levels of labor-intensive.
Yes, the creative stubbornness was real.

Early on, I resisted anything that smelled like streamlining.
I didn't want this to be *just a line.*
It had to feel like *me.*

Special. Touchable. Intentional.

I wanted people to open a package and *feel the care*—like each piece had passed through real hands.
Because it had.

Take the hang tags. I had a vision: raw edges, like something curated by a *fairy with excellent taste.*
Earthy. Magical. Definitely not mass-produced.

But nothing pre-made gave me that look.
So, I hand-tore 300 tags. Hole-punched them at 2 AM.
Top Chef reruns in the background. Glue everywhere. Slightly manic.
Weirdly proud.

Later—when we grew—I'd catch myself asking,
Why am I still doing this at 2 AM?

Some of it was pride. Some control.
Some was learning the hard way.

But I had to go through it to figure out what actually mattered—
and what I could finally let go of.

And it wasn't just the tags.

I hand-stitched tiny x's on pockets because machines weren't
personal enough.
I stitched during meetings. At lunch. In the car.
Less fashion empire, more *sweatshop-of-one.*
But it mattered.

Even when we scaled, streamlined, and started shipping more—
I still touched every design.
Whispered go be great into the seams.

Did anyone else notice?
Maybe not.

I noticed.
And that was the point.

the rise & the fall after the rise

I grew. The company grew.

Gretchen—a sharp-eyed photographer fresh out of school—landed
in my orbit.
She got it.
Not just the look, but the feeling.
She became my right hand, my rock, my friend.
We pushed each other. Dreamed loud.

Then came Barbie—publicist, firestarter, friend. A force in heels.
She believed in the brand like it was her own and never took no for
an answer.
With her beside me, the fight didn't feel so lonely.

And Robin—one of five reps, but the one who moved mountains.
Style. Hustle. Vision.
She got us into the right rooms.
She didn't just place us—she positioned us.
With her, we weren't just building a brand. We were building a family.

Soon, we were in boutiques across the U.S., Europe, and Asia.
I hit the New York trade shows two, sometimes three times a year.
Our proving ground.
The booth design, the samples, the energy—it was chaos, but it was ours.
Every piece told a story.

When buyers' eyes lit up, I felt it.
This wasn't just clothing. It was connection.

Eventually, I outgrew my one-bedroom apartment and moved into
a downtown loft.
Exposed brick. High ceilings. Racks lining the walls.
I hired my first assistant.
We set our sights on Nordstrom.

Everyone said, "Not until year two or three."
I didn't wait for permission.

I cold-called the buyer, landed the meeting, packed my samples—
fifteen pieces that looked like a hundred—
and walked out with an order and a launch event.
Outside I cried.
A few seconds of *holy shit.*

When you're bold, even the rules start bending.

This wasn't luck. It wasn't handed to me.
I built it—with instinct, caffeine, and grit.

But not every thread held.

Early on, I'd hired a production manager—
a quiet, intense Korean woman with a dream of designing kidswear.
Her studio was full of tiny garments—beautiful and ghostlike.
She was good.
Until she wasn't.

Meetings moved to parking lots. Fabrics vanished. Trust frayed.
When I confronted her, she crumbled—said I was her only friend.
That this brand gave her purpose again.
That it wasn't just mine anymore—it was hers, too.

But I had a business to run.
And the lines she crossed? I couldn't un-cross them.
I let her go.

She sued me.
Blocked access to my goods.
Held inventory hostage.

It got ugly—fast.
Court followed.

She showed up mid-breakdown—crying, shaking, unraveling in
front of the judge.
I was stunned.
And she won.

I appealed.
Months later, I won. Case dismissed.

Then came the letter—ten pages of apology, grief, and regret.
She missed working together. Wished things had gone differently.

And honestly? So did I.
She was gifted.
But the damage was done.

It broke something I didn't know could break—
but it also proved I wouldn't stay broken.

It was a brutal lesson in this strange, beautiful world
where dreams and business don't always play nice.

As I found my rhythm again, a friend introduced me to a judge-
turned-investor.

Big promises followed: go public, raise capital, trackable fabric, global
scale.
I said yes.

The money came in.
The energy built.
And then—everything stalled.

The investors were under investigation.
Fraud. Lawsuits.

I wasn't the target, but I got pulled into the wreckage.

The worst part? I'd sold shares to friends.
People who believed in me. Trusted me.
They lost money, too.
I carried that quietly—*like a bruise no one could see.*

It rattled me.
But I didn't quit.

I kept showing up.

Kept creating.
Kept clawing forward—even when the floor fell out.

Because I didn't get here by accident.
I hauled. Stitched. Sold. Dreamed.
Scandals, lawsuits, storms—
none of it could bury what I built.

Because it was never just clothes.
It was my name.
My story.
My skin in every seam.

sushi & soul

One night, I was having dinner—a casual sushi spot with a friend—
when a family walked in.
Their daughter was wearing one of our sweatshirts.

I froze.
Tears welled up.

It was real.

This thing I built—thread by thread—was out in the world.
On *her.*
Not in a showroom.
Not on a hanger.
But *living.*

It wasn't just clothing.
It was a signal.
Soft power in cotton form.
A quiet reminder: *You belong.*

Not only for her—for *me.*
For the kid I used to be.
The one who always felt a little outside.
Who just wanted to be seen.

And now?
She was showing up—stitched into sweatshirts.
Alive in color.
Chosen on purpose.

That moment changed everything.

And yet—no spotlight. No champagne.

Just me in a messy studio.
Thread stuck to my pants.
Takeout on the floor.
Half-drunk boba sweating next to my laptop.

And a thought, clear and loud: *I did that.*

No parade.
No headline.
Just proof.

The pieces were out there.
Being chosen.
Being loved.

And that was enough.

I didn't need applause—only a nap.
Maybe some carbs.

Sometimes peace doesn't look like a breakthrough.
Sometimes it's a room that's finally quiet.
And a voice inside that says:
You didn't just dream it. You delivered.

the mural & the mirror

One night, not long before everything clicked, I stood alone in my loft, staring at the wall.
Lights dim.
The silence—too sharp.

It wasn't the chaos of auditions, the rush of a new collection, or even the pressure of survival that made my pulse race—
it was the stillness.
That strange stretch after something ends but before the next thing begins.
The liminal space I always tried to skip.

I hadn't painted it alone.
One night—wine in hand, brushes flying—my friends and I covered the wall in color.
No plan.
Only instinct.

A riot of flowers and wild vines bloomed across the plaster—unruly and alive.
Like a story that didn't need to make sense to be *true*.

It reminded me of dance—
before the pressure.
The stakes.

The job.
Color without permission.
Expression without rules.
Creation that didn't have to be perfect—only *honest*.

I stood there, staring at it, and realized:
I'd spent so long chasing applause, staying busy, outrunning my own quiet—
I forgot what it felt like to make something simply *because it moved me.*

Being *on* had become a drug.
But that night, I let it wear off.
I *let the silence breathe.*
And in that stillness, something returned.

Not the old me.
The *unmasked* me.

This wasn't about the next gig.
Or the next goal.

It was about remembering the spark underneath it all.

Not the spotlight.
Not the hustle.
The joy of creating—without anyone watching.

That night, I reclaimed the pause.
And the next morning, I didn't wake up with a plan.
I woke up with *myself.*

full circle, in extra small

Funny... I landed in kids' fashion.

Of all the wild turns—cardigans, commercials, couture dreams—
it was tiny tees and toddler sleeves that stuck.
And maybe that wasn't random.

You know how therapists always talk about the inner child?
I didn't just meet mine.
She launched a brand.

The mission? Help kids embrace exactly who they are.
No hiding. No apologizing.
No sanding off the weird to blend in.
Loud? Great.
Sensitive? Even better.
A little strange? *Perfect.*

Every stitch, every pocket, every design was speaking to them—
and to me.
Saying: *You're not too much. You're the blueprint.*

Because the universe will always find a way to nudge you.
Sometimes through a breakdown.
Sometimes through a ball of yarn.

And sometimes—
through a sweatshirt on a stranger's kid in a sushi restaurant.

That's how I found her.
Not by fixing.
Not by forcing.

Just by making space.

She's right here.
A little weirder. A little wiser.
Fully herself.

Home.

✦

closed for now

Thought I was just taking a break.
Turns out, I was being rebooted.

the last fold

I had a solid run—the kind people dream of.
Press. Momentum. Stockists. A message I believed in.
I weathered storms. Chased joy. Made mistakes. Grew—
as a creative, as a human.
But something had begun to fade.

The world was moving online.
Shopping habits were changing.
The magic of real-time discovery—holding a piece, feeling its energy,
watching someone light up when it fit their kid *perfectly*—was
disappearing.
And *I felt it.*

The joy was fading.
The connection, dimming.

Now it was about speed. Scale. Curation for the scroll.
I wasn't built for viral.
And I didn't want to play that game.

What I loved most—the spark, the storytelling, the intimacy—
was being replaced by clicks and carts.
It felt hollow. *Disconnected.*

And deep in my gut, I knew:
this era was winding down.

Somewhere in that quiet—before the world roared back—
a new question arrived:
If not this... then what?

So I made the call—
to step back.
To close the chapter.

I packed the final shipment myself.
Folded each piece like it mattered.
Because it did.

Turned off the lights.
Closed the door.

No ceremony.
Just silence.
And it was enough.

the sacred pause

And then—boom. COVID hit.
The world shut down. Retail shut down. Life hit pause.

And in a strange, brutal way, it felt like confirmation.
Like the universe had been whispering—
and now it was done being *subtle*.

Everything I'd built was already winding down.
The world was just catching up.

I didn't panic. I didn't cling.
Instead of scrambling to save something that no longer brought me joy,
I chose stillness.

Not as surrender.
As strategy.
A reset.
A sacred pause.

The world went sideways.
Open. Shut. Open again.
Mask on. Mask off.
Hope rose. Hope *crashed.*

What we thought would last a few weeks turned into months. Then years.
Time got weird.
Some days crawled.
Others disappeared.

Everyone held their breath for *normal*.
But *normal* was gone—
and maybe that was the point.

For the first time in years:
No hustle.
No launches.
No brands to push.
No more performing like survival depended on it.

And in that stillness—something unlocked.
I wasn't chasing. I wasn't proving.
Just here.

At first, the quiet felt wrong.
Too slow. Too bare.
But then... I started hearing things I'd forgotten:

My own voice.
My instincts.
The steady pulse of curiosity I used to trust—
before the world got so loud.

This wasn't the end.
It was a *recalibration*.

The runway was gone.
Something new was loading.

Then—just when it felt like I could finally breathe—
the signal got weird.

We took a trip.
Cautious. Grateful. Stir-crazy.
I don't remember when it started—
maybe the airport, maybe the plane.
At first, I thought: *exhaustion.*

Then—
bam.

Knife to the ribs.
Head pounding.
Flu × 1000.
I thought I was dying.

Test after test said negative.
My body said otherwise.

I couldn't move.
Couldn't eat.
Even breathing hurt.

And just as the fog began to lift—
Positive.
COVID.

After all that time.
All those near-misses.

It didn't just tap me.
It *leveled* me.

But what stayed with me more than the fever or the pain?
The world.
And how it revealed itself—
when everything breaks.

the other virus

As an Asian woman, I saw it in their eyes.
The double takes. The flinch.
The air pulled tight.

Like maybe—*I* was the reason.
Like *I* had something to answer for.

It wasn't everyone.
But it was enough.
Enough to feel the blame before it was spoken.
Enough to know: while the virus hit the lungs—
hatred hit the gut.

Fear doesn't always yell.
Sometimes it glares.
Sometimes it steps back.
Sometimes it pretends not to look—
but *looks anyway.*

Even in a fever haze, I could read it.
In hallways. In checkout lines.
In every space where I was too close, too seen, *too other.*

This wasn't just a virus.
It was the *other* one.

The one that hides behind "jokes,"
behind silence,
behind that look that says: *you don't belong here.*

But I do.

I stayed upright.
Eyes forward.
Held my ground.

Because *visibility* isn't the threat.
Their discomfort is.

I didn't come out quieter.
I came out *clear.*

Even when it stung.
Even when they stared.
Even when the world went sideways—

I stayed *me.*
And *louder.*

Because this time, I wasn't asking to belong.
I wasn't waiting to be let in.

I saw it.
I named it.
I outlasted it.

And I let it mark me.
Not as damage—
as proof.

the build before the break

It started quietly.
A flicker. Then a hum.

After the shutdowns.
After the grief.
After the unraveling—
something in me began to click back on.

Not fully. Not fast.
But I was dreaming again.

Writing. Sketching.
Jotting ideas on napkins.
Talking TV concepts.
The wheels were turning.

I'd sit on my couch, laptop open, reaching for something—
like *possibility* had just come back into season.

For the first time in a long time, the future didn't feel like a slammed door.
It felt slightly *ajar.*

Ideas sparked.
Momentum built.

For a second, I thought: *This is it.*
The pause. The pull.
Maybe nothing was in my way.
Maybe *I* was.

I believe in timing.
In divine delays.
In the sacred pause that empties your hands for what's next.

And maybe that's what this was:
An inhale.
A signal from the universe that something new was about to begin.

I didn't know how much would have to fall away to make room for it.

Life was stirring.
Ideas were blooming.
And somewhere in my left armpit—
a plot twist was forming.

✦

rebuilt from scratch

Everything changed.
So I did too.

initiated

Life had finally calmed down enough for me to start dreaming again—
not notebook dreams.
Real ones.
The kind that hums in your gut and won't shut up.

My sister—quiet on the outside, ride-or-die inside—always backed
my wildness.
I've never played it safe.
She's never asked me to.

So I was plotting.
Imagining.
Gaining momentum.

Then I felt it.

Small.
Hard.
Pea-sized.
Tucked inside my left armpit like a secret.

I brushed it off.
Probably a cyst. Ingrown.
Something that would drain on its own.
No big deal.

Even my doctor wasn't worried.
"Let's give it a few months," she said.

So I waited.

Until lunch with a friend—deeply loved, slightly woo-woo.
A kinesiologist who reads energy like body language.
Between bites, he reached over, touched the lump, closed his eyes...

Then opened them:
"It's cancer."

Just like that.
No soft entry.
No fluff.

"Come see me Monday," he said.

The floor tilted.
My head spun.
Everything slowed.

Cancer?
No.
Not me.

I was healthy. Strong.
I'd just beat COVID.
I was careful. Controlled.
And now this?

I didn't know what it meant—
but it didn't feel like just an illness.
It felt like an *initiation.*

Not a detour.
A *plot twist.*

And the worst part?

Somewhere deep down—
I already knew.

the whirlwind

Once the test came back positive, it felt like I got strapped into a
rollercoaster I never agreed to ride.
Click. Seatbelt down. Bar across the chest. And *go.*
No stopping. No turning back. No time to process.

Scan after scan.
Appointment after appointment.
Blood work. MRIs. Biopsies. Ultrasounds.
I took more tests in three weeks than I had in my entire life.

And the needles?
I started naming my veins to cope.
Lefty was reliable. Righty had stage fright.
Veinzilla—a stubborn little diva in my forearm—never showed up
without drama.
The nurses laughed.
I wasn't joking.
I was a human pincushion.

The port in my chest didn't hurt, but it pressed—
like a weight that had overstayed its welcome.
I went numb. Not emotionally—*mentally.*
I had to check out to get through.

Because suddenly, I wasn't living in weeks or months.
I was living in *appointments*.

They mapped out my year like a military op:
chemo, surgery, radiation, more scans, more blood, follow-ups.

And the kicker?
They handed me a binder. A calendar.
Smiled like I'd just signed up for an *aggressive wellness retreat*.
Dress code? Pajamas.
Perks? Nausea, hair loss, hospital-grade snacks.

I was overwhelmed.
Exhausted.
But I showed up.

What else do you do when the ride starts?
You grip the bar.
Scream if you have to.
Laugh when you can.
Pray you don't throw up your breakfast.

Somewhere between the blood draws and biopsy results, it hit me—
this was my life now.
Not forever. But *for now.*

So I did what I've always done.
I showed up.
Mascara optional.
Sweatpants mandatory.

I joked my way through the waiting room.
Befriended the phlebotomist.
Took selfies in the hospital gown like it was *Fashion Week for the chronically brave.*

If I was going to fight for my life, I'd do it *my way*—
with grit, grace, and a little bit of glitter.

Stage 2.
It had spread—metastasized to my lymph nodes.
WTF.
I barely caught colds. Now I was here.
Lost. Confused. Scared.
In full-blown *denial.*

My kinesiologist—the one who called it before any scan—begged
me not to do chemo.
"It'll destroy you," he warned. "There are other ways."

But the doctors pushed.
And me?
I wanted it out.
I wanted to live.

So for once, I didn't buck the system.
I picked the standard route.

City of Hope.
Second opinions.
Scans. Plans.

The verdict was clear:
Start now.
It's aggressive.
Don't wait.

So I leaned on the ones who knew how to hold me through it.
My healer. My acupuncturist.
The steady hands. The quiet anchors.

My healer was calm. Fierce. Unshakable.
No platitudes. Just space.
She asked the kind of questions that peeled back the layers
without causing a mess.
She helped me come back to my body—
not just to fight, but to *forgive* it.

The acupuncturist was sharp.
Ancient meets punk rock.
She mapped my meridians, handed me bitter teas that tasted like
bark and betrayal, and said,
"Drink it all."
So I did.
Because what else do you do when your life's on the line?

They showed up.

Every three weeks.
On a schedule tighter than most friendships.
They never asked what I needed.
They simply brought it.

One day, my healer looked at me and said something I wasn't expecting—
something that landed like a *dare*.

The others echoed it in their own ways.
Different words, same message:

"Not everyone gets a second chance.
You've maxed out version one.
Time to upgrade.
This isn't just cancer—
it's a rite of passage."

A *rite of passage.*
That line hit me sideways.
Like... *okay, wow.*
No pressure.
But they weren't wrong.

So with that strangely aligned *(and slightly terrifying)* blessing,
I said,
Alright then. Let's go.

Cue dramatic music.
Cue warrior montage.
Cue snacks.
And a calendar I didn't ask for.

And in a blink—
the fight began.
With glitter in my bag.
And *grit in my bones.*

the invitation

What was this?
A cosmic interruption?
A sacred reordering?
A brutal, beautiful invitation to begin again?

How do you even prepare for something like this?
You don't.
You pick a date.
Like it's a haircut. Or a vacation.

Mine?
The week of my birthday.
What a gift.

Crystal—my best friend, my ride-or-die—threw me one last hurrah.
An early birthday celebration before I dove into the unknown.
It made me think of Paris.
Us wide-eyed and wild, chasing croissants and possibility.

We were fearless back then.
Free in the way only youth—or denial—allows.

Now here we were.
Older. Softer.

Still standing.
Showing up when it mattered.

We laughed.
We danced.
We toasted with trembling hands.

Because under the joy... was fear.
The kind that hums in your bones.

And to make things weirder—
I had started dating someone.
One month in.
New. Sweet. Uncomplicated.

What do you even say?
Hey, this has been fun. Also—I have cancer. Happy Tuesday.

But it was real.
The awkwardness.
The timing.
The honesty it demanded.

Cancer speeds everything up.
It's not about flirtation anymore.
It's about survival—
and who's willing to stand beside you in the dark.

He worked in the medical field.
So when the fog hit, I called him.
He walked me through it—calmly. Clearly.

A voice of reason when I had none.

Then I had the talk.
The one where you try to let someone off the hook.

"Thanks," I said. "This has been fun.
I don't expect you to stay.
It's going to get dark.
You'll see me at my worst."

He didn't flinch.
"Who's going to make you laugh?" he said.
Then held me tight—and took me somewhere soft.
For ice cream. For breath.

This man I barely knew... refused to leave.
He showed up.
Held my hand through the unthinkable.
Sat with me in silence.
Helped carry a weight I couldn't name yet.

Was it love?
Grace?
A gift from the universe?
Maybe all of the above.

But what I know for sure?

He stayed.

day one

The stalls looked like fitting rooms—curtains, plastic chairs, IV poles.
Each one held a body. A story. A dose.
Patient in. Poison in. Patient out. Next.
Mechanical. Efficient. Almost casual.
Like survival was just another appointment.

October 5. First infusion.
I rolled in like it was a sleepover—suitcase, snacks, false confidence.
No clue what to expect.
Only thing I could control was being ready.

Within an hour, I fired my oncologist.
She'd missed a key email—wrong info on the drugs.
Not ideal when you're choosing between poisons.
I needed someone sharper.
So—I found one.

They walked me to my stall, next to the Paxman machine.
It looked like a chair.
It was not.

Cold cap strapped on. Steroids. Ice gloves. Benadryl.
Then the freeze.
Unbearable.
My jaw locked. My body shook.

I meditated. Quietly cried. Felt ridiculous.
IV in my chest. Blankets up to my chin.
A warrior in battle gear I never asked for.

Then from behind the curtain—
a voice: soft, steady, certain.
"It's going to be okay."

I didn't know her.
But I clung to that voice like a lifeline.
She carried me through the first hour.

Tick. Tock.
The longest second hand in history.

Two stalls down, someone was blasting *Friends*.
Joey: "How you doin'?"
I had no answer.

Then—lunch delivery from hell.
Plastic bag. Rolling pole.
Bright red pouch.
The Red Devil.

Two nurses checked my wristband.
Confirmed it was me.
Watched it snake into my chest.
Fruit punch of destruction.

I chewed ice to avoid mouth sores.
A ritual. A reach for control.

Every five minutes, I swore it had to be noon.
It was 11:07.

The ice socks turned to torture.
Cold to burn to nothing.
My toes ghosted. I wiggled them. A sanity check.

Hour three or four—
I drifted.
Not asleep. Not awake.
Chemo twilight.

Dumb thoughts floated up:
Did I move the laundry?
Is Kenzi mad?
Is Charles eating a vegetable?
Is this my life now—bagged poison and blankets that felt like someone
definitely died under them?

The nurses joked.
Friends kept yelling.
And the woman from earlier?
A few stalls down now.
Reading *The Purpose-Driven Life.*
We never spoke.
But she was mine.
My chemo sister.

I tried to look cute. For no one.
Laughed—quietly.
Because... what else?

When it ended (almost), they handed me a box.
Injectables. Homework.
One shot a day, five days.
To rebuild what we'd annihilated.

Barbaric.
Brilliant.
Brutal.

I carried it out like a bomb.
Frozen. Dizzy.
Stunned this was my life now.

Outside, the sun was blinding.
Emails, errands, school pickup lines—
the world didn't skip a beat.
But I had.

That night, I lay in bed—motionless.
No more distractions.
No more performance.
The guck rising:
Bad decisions. Leftover energies. Voices that drowned me out.

This wasn't healing.
This was demolition.
Excavation.

Not meditation—exorcism.

Strip it back.
The places I stayed too long.
The damage I let carry my name.

Kill everything. Then rebuild.
That was the plan.
Not only in my blood—
in my life.

I wasn't surviving.
I was clearing the wreckage.

A thought slipped in:
What if I don't wake up tomorrow?

And weirdly—I didn't panic.
I simply wondered:
Would I be okay with that?

Pain meds. Toilet.
3 a.m. haze.

Back in bed, it hit me—
This is only the beginning.

cancer? same.

When people hear the word cancer, their first instinct is strangely universal.
They press their ribs. Rub their necks.
Scan their bodies like it might be hiding somewhere—waiting for an invite.

We think everyone's watching us.
But really?
Most people are busy staring at their own reflections,
wondering if *they're next.*

That's exactly what happened when I told my sister.

Outwardly composed. Inwardly spiraling.
That night, she checked herself too.
The next morning—
"Okay, don't freak out... but I found a lump."

I rolled my eyes.
"You're being dramatic. You're fine."

Then she went to the doctor.

Stage 0.
Borderline cancer.

No chemo—but a lumpectomy. Radiation.
The quieter version of the same road.
It felt like she couldn't let me go through it alone.
So she didn't.

She stayed close.
Matched me in spirit, if not meds.
Like only a sister could.

No declarations. No pep talks.
Pure presence.

She picked me up. Got me soup.
Offered silence when I couldn't talk
and conversation when I needed distraction.

We didn't say much about the fear, the what-ifs.
But there was something unspoken.
A pact without words.

And I'll never forget that.

Because when the world was spinning—
she didn't try to stop it.
She stood still beside me.

No pity. No drama.
Only the quiet kind of badass loyalty that says:
I'm here. Now what?

and again (and again)

Then the next day appears.
Uninvited. Unapologetic.
The sun rises—oblivious to the war in my body.

And it continues.
The ache. The fog.
The parade of pills.
The sideways glances in the mirror—because even I don't recognize
myself.

Week one: I move like glass.
Wince at noises.
Whisper to my organs.
Coax my appetite with toast and bone broth—
soft things that require no trust.

Week two: the clouds lift, barely.
I do laundry.
Text someone back.
Eat half a sandwich.

Week three: I feel strong.
I might walk.
Lip gloss, a tiny ritual of return.
Almost believe I'm getting my life back.

And then—*bam.*
Back in the chair.
Same room. Same cap. Same cold.
Same Red Devil, marked with an X.

Another gut punch.
Another surrender.
Another spin on the carousel of collapse.

It's *insanity.*
And we start over.
Again. Then again. *Relentlessly.*

The hardest part isn't the pain.
It's the *disorientation.*

Time dissolves.
You lose the day.
Lose yourself.

Everything blurs.
Mornings bleed into afternoons,
into nights of partial sleep
and looping thoughts—like a bad song you didn't choose.

Somewhere in there, your mind checks out.
Books a one-way flight to *anywhere but here.*
And your body clocks in.
Pumped full of chemicals.
Expected to bounce back like a good little soldier.

You become two people:
The one who jokes with nurses and says, *I'm fine, thanks*—
and the one inside, *screaming*.

You try to hope.
But *hope is fragile here.*
Like a balloon on a windy day.
You hold it tight, terrified it'll float away if you look down.

So you keep going.
Not because you're brave—
but because there's *no other option.*

Some days I believed I was healing.
Other days, I just prayed the poison was killing the cancer
faster than it was killing me.

Kill the cancer.
Try not to kill me in the process.
That was the deal.

pretty on tuesday, prayer by friday

My agent and I made a quiet pact: one day at a time.
Work... while going through treatment.
"Other clients had done it," she said.
So why not me?

After the first infusion, I felt invincible.
Steroids kicking. Glowing. Energized.
I looked incredible. I felt incredible.
Maybe I can do this.
Maybe it won't be so bad.

The next day—I booked a job.
I cried—happy tears in the middle of darkness.
Proof there was some sparkle. Still possibility in the wreckage.

We believed the window between rounds would be enough:
heal, bounce back, repeat.
I had hope.

It was the calm before the collapse.

Then it hit.
The crash.
Everything they warn you about—
and everything they don't.

My face erupted.
Pustules. Flare-ups. Raw, oozing skin. A mask of fire.
Nausea. Diarrhea. No taste buds.
Food became a texture game.

And I had a fitting to get to.

As a dancer, you're trained to show up.
The curtain rises. You go.
So I did.
From glow-up to gut punch.
Three days flat.

I begged for meds.
My doctor pushed back.
"What's more important," he asked, "a job—or your life?"

I couldn't answer.
Not with my face on fire and my calendar staring back at me.

So I pleaded.
"Please—this one time. Then I'll stop. I'll rest."

He agreed. Reluctantly.

It wasn't the pain alone.
It was the loss of normalcy.
Of dignity. Of the face I used to know.

I picked up the prescription. And I prayed.
Not some polished prayer—
the kind that comes from the pit.

Please let it work.
Let me show up Tuesday with peace.
With a face I recognize.
Give me a few more days to feel like me.

Charles held my hand. Soft. Steady. No judgment.
He didn't say much.
But he stayed.

And still—loss found a way in.

The cold cap helped,
but I could feel things shifting.
My hair felt fragile—
like one wrong move might send it packing.

My body was changing.
Ready or not.

the job that nearly broke me

I made it through the fitting. Barely.
A mask bought me time—thank God it was still normal post-COVID.
No one questioned it. One more layer between me and the world.
Like armor.

Then came the shoot.
Car commercial.
Malibu.
A few people knew. The stylist helped hide the port.

To the hair person, I whispered,
"Hey... a little heads-up—be gentle. My hair might bail mid-brush."
She froze. Then nodded, like this wasn't her first rodeo in the
cancer trenches.
"Got it," she said, already adjusting her grip. "Magic hands only."

That one line made me smile.
Even in the absurdity, there were still humans—kind, unbothered,
quietly heroic—helping me hold it together.

At least I was sitting in the scene.
No choreography. No running on the beach.
Me in a car.
A miracle—because walking, moving, existing at that point? *Already
too much.*

I was wrecked. Holding on by a thread.
But I made it through.
Hit my marks.
Smiled when they needed me to.
Breathed through the ache like it was scripted.

Then I got home... and passed out.
Slept for two days straight.
Body down. Spirit empty.

And after all of that?
The commercial never even aired.

What was the lesson?
Honestly—I don't know.
Strength? Endurance?
The price of pushing through when my body's waving a white flag?

Maybe it was just life.
Unfair. Unscripted. Unclear.

Not every chapter teaches you something.
Some are messes—ugly, unearned.
No redemption. No arc. No closure.
Only pain, paperwork, and a bill for parking.

And maybe that's the point.
Not to make it meaningful.
To survive it.

I didn't want a phoenix moment.
I wanted my damn energy back.
Skin that didn't scream. Hair that didn't bail.
I wanted my plans. My peace.
And maybe a smoothie that didn't taste like metal.

But no.
All I got was a ghost gig and a box of chemo homework.

And when I snapped?
It wasn't elegant. It wasn't profound.
It was a loud, *This is fucking bullshit!*
To the mirror. To the ceiling. To the whole universe.

And for once—I didn't try to reframe it.
Didn't gratitude-journal it into a lesson.
Didn't pretend the rage meant something noble.

It just was.
Ugly. Honest. Necessary.

Because sometimes, survival isn't about finding meaning.
It's about not letting the bullshit win.

the shedding

It started small.
A strand here. A strand there.
Pillow. Shower. Hoodie.
Like my hair was plotting a slow escape.

The crown went first. *Classic.*
A cruel nod to male-patterned baldness.
I stared at it in the mirror like—*Really? That's where we're starting?*

I clung to the cold cap like it was a magical helmet.
As if freezing my scalp hard enough might let me keep what was left.

The irony? I once shaved my head on purpose.
Back then, it was *power.*
Now? I was begging to keep what I used to give away.

Funny how survival rewrites the rules.

By round four, I was ready to tap out.
The cap was *torture.*
I asked the nurse, "How much longer?"
She smiled like a hostage negotiator. "You've got this."

I didn't.

I asked for stronger meds. Got them. Popped them. Braced for battle.

Each shower felt like roulette.
Each clump, a quiet loss.
The cold cap helped, but the shedding came anyway—strand by strand.
Even with prayers, meds, and ice packs, my body had its own plan.

Was it vanity? *Of course.*
But not *just* vanity.
It was identity. Safety.
A veil between me and the world.

Eventually, the shame dissolved.
And underneath it?
Something truer. Meaner. *Braver.*

I shed old fears. Old stories. Old definitions of beauty.

Losing my hair stripped more than aesthetics.
It stripped the *mask.*

And what was left?

Mine. All mine.

Not about what I lost—
but what I *found.* And *claimed.*

body rewritten

But the hair was just the headline—
I lost the body I knew.
The one I had danced with. Performed with. *Survived* with.

Chemo made it foreign.
Bloated. Raw. Weak.
My skin freaked out. Muscles vanished.
Even my walk changed—like my body forgot the choreography.

It felt like *betrayal.*
First for growing the cancer.
Then by breaking down while trying to survive it.

But over time, I stopped seeing betrayal.
Started seeing a *rewrite.*

The old body was built on precision.
Perfection. *Performance.*
This one? Built on pain.
Persistence.
Power.

Not a bounce-back body.
An *I'm still standing* body.
An *I fought for this* body.

And I started to love her—
not for how she looked in jeans,
but for how she held me *through hell.*

Scars became landmarks.
Proof of survival.
Of softness that didn't mean weakness.
Of beauty that didn't need permission.

Femininity got redefined.
Not lashes or curves or algorithm-approved perfection.
This was *earned.*
Raw.
The kind you meet in the dark.

Softness inside strength.
Letting someone care for me.
Asking for help.
Letting love in.

I used to measure beauty in inches and angles.
Now it's presence.
Warmth.
The ability to laugh while holding pain in the same breath.

My body didn't fail me.
She stayed.
Adapted.
Wrote a new story—
and dared me to live it.
She's softer now.

A little wilder.

Still here.

Mascara optional. Sweatpants earned.

surgery day

After the first round of chemo, the lump vanished.
Just... *poof.* Like it got bored and ghosted.

I should've felt victorious.
But the war wasn't over.

Next up: surgery.
And because the universe has a dark sense of humor,
it was scheduled for *Valentine's Day.*
The national holiday of heart-shaped bullshit—
and I was headed into a freezing OR to get my chest sliced open.
Romantic.

The procedure? *Textbook.*
Clean margins. Five lymph nodes.
Everyone was thrilled.

Except me.

I woke up in full meltdown mode—
hives everywhere, scratching like a raccoon in heat,
snapping at nurses like they personally betrayed me.

"Ma'am, we need you to move along."

Move along?
I'd just been carved up and medically gift-wrapped.
Wheeled down a hallway like *abandoned luggage.*

I lost it.
Everything went fuzzy—fluorescent lights, static voices, blind rage.
I remember clawing at my arms and thinking:
This? This cannot be my love story.

No chocolates. No roses.
Just fentanyl and a full-body histamine revolt.

It wasn't brave.
It wasn't cinematic.
It was primal.
Unfiltered.
Ugly in the most *honest way.*

Somewhere in that haze, I was trying to find my way back to *me.*
Not the stitched-up version.
Not the loopy, hospital-gown extra.

Me.
Whatever was left beneath the scrubs and surgical tape.

There are no Hallmark cards for this kind of love—
rashy, puffy-faced, post-op love that says:
"Don't move. We're not finished."

The kind of love that doesn't arrive with flowers.
It shows up with crackers.
Waits through the silence.
Touches your arm when you forget where you are.
And stays—when you want to disappear.

what got me through

Sometimes it wasn't anything profound.
A dumb meme mid-infusion that made me laugh-snort through the
nausea.
Or Charles—showing up with yet another pair of shoes.
He had this theory: *if it sparkled, maybe it could ward off doom.*
At the very least, distract me from the war raging in my bloodstream.

Before every infusion, I stole a shirt from his closet.
Didn't matter which one—just that it smelled like him.
A little armor. A little comfort.
Something real when everything else felt rigged.

And Kenzi?
Curled up against my leg like a furry little sandbag of judgment.
Silent. Heavy. Hyper-aware.
Her vibe? *You good?*
With a side of *Get it together.*

Some days, that was enough.
Not inspiration. Not perspective.
Just something alive beside me.
Something that didn't ask me to be strong.

So I got back in the chair.
Not because I believed in silver linings.

Not because I felt powerful.
Because pain and I go way back—
and I knew how to show up for a fight,
even when every part of me said, *enough.*

Charles brought the shoes.
Kenzi kept watch.
My sister checked in like clockwork.
And me?
I clutched my borrowed armor, muttered something sarcastic,
and let the poison in.

Because sometimes surviving isn't brave.
It's *pissed-off.*
Splintered.
Over it—
and *still here.*

rebirth

This isn't just about surviving cancer.
It's about reclaiming self—
with rage, humor, and zero interest in softening the truth.

Six rounds of chemo. One lumpectomy. Fifteen rounds of radiation.
Ongoing infusions to close out the year.

I marked each one like a prisoner etching lines on a wall—
counting down,
waiting for the moment I could say: *I'm done.*

And eventually... I was.

Treatment wrapped right before my 50th birthday.
A milestone. A finish line.
It was a beginning disguised as an ending.

But instead of relief, there were questions:
Now what?
Who am I now?
Where do I even start?

I looked in the mirror and barely recognized myself.
Frail. Foggy. Ten years older. Bald spots. No lashes.
Like I'd been dragged across a battlefield—

and somehow spit back out upright.
Wobbly. Bruised. But standing.

Reentry was weird.
The fog lingered.
My brain glitchy—thoughts scattered, words slippery.
One foot in, one foot somewhere else.

Chemo brain is real.
So is healing.
So is the disorientation no one claps for.

My body was back.
My focus wasn't.
And if I'm honest—*neither was I.*

You wait.
You adjust to the fog.
Start thinking: *maybe this is just how it stays now.*

And then—quietly—it lifts.

Thoughts returned.
The ground steadied.
And suddenly—you're here.

Frayed. Unfinished.
Present.

Getting healthy again felt like climbing stairs in the dark.
Every step unsure.
Every win fragile.

People smiled, congratulated me—"You did it!"
But inside, I kept thinking:
Did I?
Am I here yet?

Normal didn't feel normal.
I was technically me—but rewired.
Softer in some places.
Sharper in others.

Finding my way back meant building a new map from scratch.
Piece by piece.
Breath by breath.

One morning, stitched with hope and caffeine,
I caught my reflection—
sweats, hoodie, sleep lines—
and smirked.

Still cute.

Didn't flinch. Didn't wince.
Just nodded like: *Alright. We're back.*

Once again, standing at the beginning.
Not broken. Not brand-new.
Rewritten.

No blueprint.
No costume.
No choreography.
No role to play but my own.

The old Taira was gone.
So who's this?

This is Taira 2.0.

Cancer didn't give me a new identity.
It burned the noise down
so I could hear the one that had been whispering underneath all along.

Not who I was.
Not yet who I'm becoming—
but wholly mine.

Because this wasn't just survival.
It was reclamation—
loud, laced with humor, and entirely mine.

reentry

You finish the climb—
and realize there's no summit. *Just sky.*

I rang the bell at the end of treatment—
that big, symbolic moment everyone talks about.

And you know what?
I felt... nothing.
Not joy. Not relief. Just awkward.

The nurse clapped, someone cheered,
and I stood there thinking—
Cool. Can I go home now?

For a year, cancer had been my job.
Brutal—but structured.
A full-time calendar of scans, meds, infusions, side effects.
Purpose, whether I wanted it or not.

And then—silence.

No more alarms.
No lab coats.
No one telling me where to be
or what to wear.

I should've felt free.
Instead—I was untethered.

Like the understudy who trained for battle...
only to be dismissed without fanfare.

Juice cleanse?
5K?
Screenplay?
Nap??

I survived the worst—
and now I was pacing the living room in sweatpants,
reorganizing the junk drawer
like it might explain what the hell comes next.

Purpose? Gone.
Structure? Gone.
That all-hands-on-deck, *keep her alive* energy? Gone.

So yeah, I rang the bell.
Then I sat in my car and cried for reasons I couldn't name.

Grief? Relief? Who knows.
Maybe just my body finally exhaling.

No soundtrack.
No breakthrough.
Just stillness—
and me learning how to breathe again.

No one tells you what to do after the bell stops echoing.
Turns out—
that's when the real work begins.

the secret I carried

There's one thing I don't say out loud very often:
I never told my parents.

They had enough to carry—
stress, health issues, aging bodies.
This would've broken them.

So I held it quietly.
Not out of shame.
Out of protection.

I had seen fear in my father once.

He was visiting me in L.A.,
en route to Thailand to see my grandmother in the hospital.
"I don't want to go," he said. "I'm scared."

It stunned me.
My dad didn't say things like that. Not out loud. Not to me.

"Then don't," I said.
But he went anyway.

I drove him to the airport.
We didn't say much. Just sat in it.

There's a part of the terminal—right past security—
where I stopped and watched him walk away.
He didn't look back.

The air stopped moving.
Time slowed.
And even though I didn't know what was coming,
something in me did.

He landed and went straight to the hospital.
Not to visit—
to be admitted.

Chest tight. Struggling to breathe.
Straight into surgery. Triple bypass.

My mom called while I was on a date.
I stayed at the table. Smiled. Ate.
Laughed at the right moments—
even though *I had left the moment entirely.*

That's what I do sometimes.
Leave.
Float above it.
Disappear, body present, mind gone.

And every time I walk past that gate at the airport, I cry.
Not loud. Not long.
But from somewhere deep.

Because a piece of me lives there.
Watching him walk away.
His voice: "I'm scared."
Mine: "Then don't."

The doctor gave him ten years.
A monk gave him twenty.
He beat both.

And somehow—that makes me angry.

Not at the survival.
At the stamp. The sentence.
That someone handed a deadline to a man still trying to breathe.
And that he carried it like luggage no one else could see.

A cardiologist and a monk handing out expiration dates?
Come on.

He made it. He's here.
Joking. Reviewing every meal like it's Michelin-rated.
Making my mom nuts—in all the usual ways.

I didn't want to do that to them.
Didn't want to hand them fear they couldn't put down.

So I didn't tell them.
And don't plan to.

Some things are too heavy to pass along—
even to the people you love.
Sometimes, silence is how we protect them.

And my friends? Troopers.
Snacks, playlists, bad jokes at chemo.
They knew when to text, when to talk,
and when to just sit beside the wreckage.

Healing doesn't happen in isolation.
It happens in community.
In the grace of being seen—
messy, bald, and fully human.

And when no one else was around?
Kenzi. My four-legged shadow.
No words. No performance. Just there.
Like she got the memo: *Be here. Don't blink.*

We got through it. Somehow.

And when the next birthday rolled around,
this time—we celebrated.
Loudly. Without fear.

Because I wasn't just alive.
I was *living.*

the myth of done

They say if you make it to five years... you've made it.
Cue the confetti. Roll credits. Cancer-free.

But what they don't tell you?
The in-between holds all the mess—and all the meaning.

Now every twinge, every cough, every random ache
triggers a silent spiral.

Normal rib pain or terminal?
Residual lump or leftover trauma?
Two sneezes or two weeks to live?

I survived the war...
and now I'm afraid of the paper cuts.

But here's what I'm learning:
You can't live in fear of what might happen.
You'll miss *what is* happening.

And what's happening now—
is life.

Messy. Miraculous. Slightly ridiculous.

So no—I don't want to spend the next five years holding my breath.
I want to spend them dancing. Laughing.
Wearing the weird outfit.
Holding the hand of someone who gets it.

Because cancer taught me this:

We don't get to choose what breaks us.
But we *do* get to choose what we build from the pieces.

And me?
I'm building something beautiful.
Even if it's lopsided.
Even if I haven't figured it out yet.

Weird. Wired.
Here.

Very much alive.

love in the realest form

On the other side of all this—was Charles.
No theatrics. No sympathy show.
Calm, steady love.

He rubbed my back. Helped with injections.
Carried groceries. Fed me when I couldn't lift a fork.
Laughed with me—even when everything else felt like hell.

He reached for humor—not to sugarcoat, but to survive.
Laughter's the only way to punch back.

He reminded me:
Love doesn't live in the mirror.
It lives in the grit. The mess. The unfiltered middle.
It doesn't perform. It doesn't run.
It holds.

And when I had nothing left—he leaned in.

Charles helped me shed armor I didn't know I had.
Didn't let me spiral too long.
Didn't let me host a pity party *without a fire exit*.
He kept me moving.

We golfed—me whipping the cart like a getaway car,
heckling him like it was the Masters.
Somewhere between the sand traps and snack breaks—we got hooked.
Accidentally. Unapologetically.

At first, I clung to the script:
Be cool. Don't need too much. Keep the chaos cute.

He didn't buy it.

He didn't want the version I'd learned to polish.
He wanted the raw reel.
The full mess.
The backstage pass with broken set pieces and mascara stains.

And the wildest part?
It started with a phone call.
Not a swipe. Not a DM.
A phone call.

Truth? *I didn't even want to go.*
Jenny—my hairstylist-slash-matchmaker-slash-sneaky genius—said,
"I know someone. You'd like him."

I rolled my eyes.
She let it go—for eight months.
Then texted him anyway.

"I had a feeling," she said. "Don't be mad."
I wasn't.
She wasn't wrong.

He called. I ignored it.
He called again.

A quick dinner turned into eight hours.
No filler. No small talk.
A conversation that felt like it had already started.

Later, he told me,
"I reminded myself—don't just look at her. Feel her."

And he did.
He really did.
He saw me—skin flaring, hair thinning, body wrecked—
when I couldn't even look at myself.

One day—mid-flare, barely holding it together—he took me shopping.
I froze. Couldn't breathe. Couldn't face the world.

"Scared?" he asked.
I nodded.

"Then stay close," he said.
"Hold my hand. Fuck what people think. It's just you and me."

No big moment. No sweeping music.
Only him grabbing my hand like panic was part of the plan.

He didn't retreat.
He didn't fix.
He stayed.

That kind of steady?
Hard to find.
Harder to keep.

a little crooked, still cute

One morning—maybe third or fourth grade—I was feeling myself.
Pink dress. Ruffled hem. Full strut. Main character energy.

Until I looked down.
Hem: unraveled.
Thread: dangling.
Dress: drooping—like it had fully given up on life.

Cue instant shame spiral.
"My dress is ruined," I told my mom, like the world was ending at
8:07 a.m.

She didn't blink.
Pulled the car over, took off a massive gold brooch—part jewelry, part
medieval weapon—and said,
"Hold still."

She pinned the hem right there in the front seat.

The brooch was so heavy it dragged the dress even lower.
I looked like a deflated cupcake in crisis.

But she grinned.
"There. Still cute."

That was her.
Make it work. Keep it moving.
Thai MacGyver with a purse full of miracles
and zero tolerance for whining.

That purse could fix a hem, cure a cough,
and feed a family of four.

It was one of those ridiculous little moments that sticks—
not because it was perfect,
but because it was *her.*
Resourceful. Calm. Maximum brooch.

I think about our dance-day routine—
driving to Reno, me rehearsing, then Sizzler.
Our sacred ritual.

I'd stack my salad bar plate like an architectural feat:
ranch, croutons, Jell-O,
and whatever mystery pasta was congealing under the sneeze guard.
Not elegant. Not even sanitary.
But it felt like love.

She didn't always say *I love you.*
But I felt it.

In the drives.
The snacks.
The giant brooch on my limp little dress.

Her way of saying:
You're covered.
A little crooked.
Still showing up.
And absolutely, undeniably cute.

behind the curtain, beside me

Some people are with you for a season.
A chapter.
A stall curtain away.

My chemo sister and I barely met in the real world—
except once.
After it was over, we went out for a drink.
To celebrate.
To breathe different air.
To toast surviving hell with our humor (somehow) intact.

But the rest?
It was endured side by side.
Same appointment times. Same IV drip. Different snacks.
A stranger, then a comfort, then someone who made me laugh
while poison slid through our veins.

We swapped side effect hacks like seasoned pros.
Held space when the Benadryl hit.
Judged the hospital snacks.
Tried to sync our nausea like it was a group project.

I brought cupcakes for her birthday.
Sang terribly. She laughed anyway.

And those Bible verses...
I wasn't religious—
Still not.
But I read them—because from her,
they felt like low-key blessings with emoji flair.

We had that drink.
Looked each other in the eye.
Said: *We made it.*

Because sometimes the people who get you through hell
aren't meant to stay forever.
They show up exactly when you need them.
And that's enough.

So wherever you are—Chemo Sister, Woman Behind the Curtain—
thank you.

You made it bearable.
You made it weird.
You made it human.

One joke, one drip, one terrible snack at a time.

kenzi, obviously

Kenzi would just stare at me.
Not in the *feed me* way—
more like *I know you're not fine, but I'll let you pretend.*

She has a look—that signature stare, full of read-every-thought energy.
Equal parts concern, judgment, and ride-or-die loyalty.
No questions. No commentary.
Just quiet presence.

She'd follow me from room to room,
flop down with a sigh,
or post up on the bed like head of security.
Always on duty. Always watching.

But don't let the soulful eyes fool you—
she's not just some mystical emotional support sidekick.

Kenzi has range.
Wild when she wants.
Sweet when snacks show up.
She knows dinner hits at 4:00 p.m. sharp—
and will sit, unblinking, at 3:59 like *tick tock, lady.*

Bossy. Cuddly. A little extra.
Basically me, but wiser.

Sometimes I look at her and think—
How did I end up with a dog that's just me in fur?
A tiny therapist with four legs
and zero tolerance for bullshit.

No words. No applause.
Steady. Silent. Slightly judgy—
but full of love.

The kind of love that doesn't flinch when you fall apart.
The kind that says:
I see you. I've got you. Now seriously—go make dinner.

So to Kenzi—
my fuzzy little mirror,
reluctant nurse,
and snack-time alarm clock—
thank you
for keeping me grounded,
slightly scolded,
and completely seen.

You always understood.

final thought - from scratch

Burn it down.
Begin again.

Not polished. Not perfect.
But real.

This isn't a comeback.
It's reconstruction —
voice, body, self.

Built from wreckage.
Stitched with rage and humor,
carried by a refusal to vanish.

✦

still writing

There's no final draft. Only a better version of truth.

yes to all of it

There were loves along the way—
fast-burning, heart-thumping, teach-me-something kinds of loves.
Beautiful disasters.
Wild beginnings with no endings worth keeping.
Great stories—not great partners.

Maybe no one made me want to stay—because I wasn't ready.
Maybe I needed time on my own to build something solid first.

At the time, I called it chemistry.
But really, it was trauma cosplaying as attraction.

To be fair, it wasn't all them.
People meet you where you are.
And if those were the mirrors I was attracting—
yeah, I had some work to do.

Also—I never swiped. Not once.
I believed in the avocado moment.
Two hands, one fruit, instant eye contact.
A gas station glance.
A glitch in the produce aisle.

Not some guy fluent in sarcasm. Or holding a fish.
I wanted fate, not filters.
A spark—not a shared hatred of cilantro.

Call me a romantic, but I wanted the collision.
The breath that forgets how to behave.
The moment that doesn't need a caption—
because your whole body already knows.

As for kids—
that story never unfolded the way I imagined.

I made a choice—early on.
No regrets. But I do wonder.
Was it timing? Karma? Or a door that quietly closed?

Then I met Charles.
And for the first time, I would've tried—with him.
Not out of pressure. Not to chase something I'd missed.
But because love felt calm. Solid.
Like something to build on, not bend for.

I even looked into freezing eggs right before treatment.
I was older. The odds weren't great. But I wanted to try.
Not to chase an old dream—
to honor what was quietly taking root.

But cancer made the call.
Maybe it was fate.
Maybe just bad timing.

Still, life gave me something to mother.

Somehow, I ended up in the world of children.
Designing for them. Dressing them.
Imagining the wild, joyful little spirits who might wear what I made.

I didn't get to clothe my own child.
But I got to clothe childhood.
And that's something.

I didn't have kids—
but I mothered dreams.
Nurtured visions.
Built things that asked for everything—and gave something back.

And that counts.

When I was a kid, I swore that when I got married, the earth would stop spinning.
Fireworks. Headlines. Possibly a national holiday.

Now? Life doesn't stop.
It doesn't wait for your big moment.

It hums in the ordinary.
It breathes in quiet wins.
The imperfect arrivals.

Marriage, kids, the "big event"?
They don't define success anymore.

Somewhere along the way, I stopped chasing a single moment to
make me whole.

I found joy in what already exists—
friends who feel like family,
work that fills me up,
love that doesn't need a spotlight.

The big events may be on their way.
But they won't be the whole story.

Not the plan I pictured—better in some ways, messier in others.
But it's the life I chose.

And that's more than okay.

I'll be over here—grateful for all of it.
Even the plot twists I never auditioned for.

clean slate, open sky

Looking back now? I laugh.
At the twists. The plot holes. The haircuts I thought would fix
everything.
At the ones who entered like main characters,
and ghosted like bad Wi-Fi. Mid-episode. No warning.

Turns out, it all added up.
Even the awkward. Especially the awkward.
Every detour, disaster, *What was I thinking?*
Shoved me exactly where I needed to go.

Joy isn't that complicated.
We act like it's a riddle, but most of the time, it's stupidly simple:
a good snack, a dumb joke,
someone who remembers how you take your coffee.

And this book?
Memoir. Fever dream. Emotional breadcrumb trail.
Whatever it is, something said: *Go back.*
So I did.

I dug through the grit, the gold, the wreckage.
Cried. Cackled. Cringed.
And thought—*Yep. That tracks.*

If I had to sum it up in one word? *Yes.*
Yes to the mess.
Yes to the magic.
Yes to wrong turns, right people, missed exits, and late bloomers.

Yes to chaos with context.
To new chapters. No roadmaps. Coffee that tastes like freedom.
Yes to Kenzi, curled up like a tiny, judgy guru.
Yes to no bra, no plans—and still being here.

More to build.
More joy to find.
More nonsense to navigate.

This feels like sky.

the surrender

For most of my life, I believed a simple lie:
If I just worked harder, pushed more, stayed sharp—
I could outrun the chaos. Control the outcome. Shape the story.
Bend life to my will like a *bossy little wizard with a planner.*

And honestly?
It worked.
For a while.

But that wasn't freedom.
It was survival in a power blazer.
Perfection as armor.
Performance as strategy.

I nailed the part. Hit my marks. Smiled through the burnout—
until even I couldn't keep up with the role.

Then came the plot twist no spreadsheet could fix:
Cancer.

At first, it felt like life ripped everything out of my hands.
But over time, I saw it for what it was—
a forced off-ramp.
A cosmic smackdown.
A full-body *sit your ass down* from the universe.

This wasn't giving up.
It was handing over the mic.
Trusting something bigger.
Letting go—for real this time.

Because here's the punchline:
The best things in my life didn't show up when I chased them.
They walked in when I stopped auditioning.
When I got quiet.
When I quit performing.
When I finally left the damn door open.

I spent years trying to force the future into shape.
But surrender doesn't work like that.
You can't *manifest by muscling*.
You can't *fast-forward* divine timing.

I had to stop gripping.
And actually—let go.

And the universe?
It's got jokes.
It'll reroute you fast—especially when you think you've got it handled.

Maybe freedom was never in the plan.
Maybe it's been hiding in the surrender the whole time.

I stopped chasing the story—
and started listening for what wanted to be written next.

the soft surprise

And then there was Charles.
Not just during treatment—
but *after*.

When the dust settled, the adrenaline wore off, the meds ran out,
and I was left blinking at the ceiling, wondering how to *human*
again—
let alone flirt.

I tried to reboot *Cool Girl Mode*™:
chill, low-maintenance, emotionally aloof.
It lasted five minutes.

He clocked the performance—and chose *presence over pretense*.
No notes. No nudges.
Just a kind of quiet that felt like *safety*.

He didn't flinch at glitchy, snacky, spiraling-on-a-Tuesday me—
like dating an emotional tumbleweed was a reasonable life choice.

He cooked.
I hovered, providing unsolicited commentary like it was my job.

Movie nights became ritual:
blanket, snacks, something streaming,

and a shared delusion that we were paid to have strong opinions
about cinematography.
I'd fall asleep halfway through.
He never said a word. Just saved me a plate.

And when the credits rolled, he'd turn and say,
"Babe. Rub my feet?"

Which—obviously—I did.
Because real love is emotional support
and massaging someone's crusty ankle at 10:42 p.m.

That's the thing about love:
It's not about declarations.
It's knowing your weird sauce order,
it's handing you a warm plate like it's sacred.
No microwave—he'd never.

Love didn't sound like violins.
It sounded like:
"I saved you the crunchy part. Eat before it gets weird."

And in a world that once demanded performance—
this felt like peace.

And honestly?
That kind of love?
Chef's kiss.

glimmers & gut checks

I've always believed in signs.
Little nudges. Cosmic winks.
The kind that hit mid-scroll or mid-bite and whisper—*pay attention, bitch.*

I see numbers everywhere now. 11:11, 3:33, 5:55.
Like the universe has a group chat—and I finally started replying.

Not superstition. *Signal.*
That twinge in your gut before your brain catches up.

Weird glimmers? *More than a few.*

Like the time I kept blanking on a music video take—over and over—
until I stopped, turned mid-scene, and locked eyes with the director.
The energy cleared.
(He asked me out after. I said yes. *Obviously.*)

Paused a show. Some guy caught my eye. Googled him.
A week later, I walked into a restaurant and there he was, pouring
my drink.
I nearly choked.

And then there was the dream—me, behind a velvet curtain, heart
pounding, lights hot.

I couldn't see the audience, but I knew they were out there.
A few weeks later, I was onstage performing at the Oscars.
Not coincidence—just a head start.

I call it alignment.
The gut knows before the plan does.

Glimmers don't shout.
They tap your shoulder. Brush your ribs.

Now—I listen.
When I get that flicker of *maybe*, I follow.

Because I've lived enough life to know:
Signs are real.
Timing's a flirt.
And the universe?
She's chaotic. She's messy.
But she always delivers.

Keep whispering, universe.
I'm not just awake—
I'm ready.

made anyway

I kept making things.
Not for work. Not for sale.
To prove I still could.

After I buzzed it off, the stares came.
So did the questions.
"Did you lose a bet?"
"Is it for a role?"
"Are you okay?"

I didn't explain.
What was I supposed to say?
Stylish. Healing. Just out here existing—appreciate your concern.

Walking into rooms, I used to tense—
wondering if I'd pass the test:
soft enough, strong enough, woman enough.

Then I stopped.
I walked in.

Hair or no hair.
Approval or not.
I was still me.
And people adjusted—*because I didn't.*

Some things I made to sell—cropped bombers with wild prints,
fringe hoodies, sequin skirts.
Others? I made just to remind myself I had a say.

No deadline. No launch.
A hat because the yarn felt good.
A script I never showed.
A shirt I wore anyway.

Tiny things. Quietly sacred.
Like that wall of wild color—painted for no one, just because we could.

Turns out—creating without permission is its own kind of power.

Art's cheaper than therapy.
And louder than silence.

still writing

I don't have all the answers.
But I kept showing up—making, listening, healing.
And somehow—that was enough.

The road didn't look like I pictured.
The wins weren't always loud.
The losses didn't always announce themselves.
But I stayed in it.
Learned to live in the in-between.
To trust the quiet.
To stop waiting for clarity to anoint something real.

There were detours I never saw coming.
Pain I didn't sign up for.
Moments I almost tapped out.

But also—
joy that snuck in anyway.
Love that didn't need fixing.
Glimmers that hit like proof in the dark.

Even now—some days—I think about that agent who said,
"Make it easier."

Tiaraya became Taira.
Syllables trimmed.
Edges sanded.
Identity, streamlined.

I became the short version.
The cooler version.
The joke version.
Tarayaki. Taramisu.

Improv identity. Inside joke. Survival skill.
But maybe that was always the game:
Rewrite. Rename. Reclaim.

And Charles?
The one I reach for.
The one reaching back.
Still holding my hand like it's front row to something sacred.

And me?
Strange. Stubborn.
Delightfully unhinged—
and yep, *still writing.*

That barista might've been right.

Maybe this was the one I was always meant to write.

The story that started with a lump—but was never really about the lump.
The one where shit hits the fan, the script gets scrapped—and
somehow,

that's when it all begins.
Not a perfect story.
Not a finished one.
But a damn good one.

Mine.

So yeah—maybe I'll take that coffee to go.
The page keeps turning.
The pen's in my hand.

And if you think I'm done—
Plot twist pending.

A few seeds are already sprouting.

Special thanks to Lion's Mane—
the mushroom that quietly rebooted my soul.
Weird. Beautiful. Effective.

TO MY PARENTS—

Thank you for the sacrifices I saw—and the ones I didn't.
For the quiet strength you carried in your bones, wore on your faces,
and passed down without ever needing to name it.

TO MY SISTER—

Thank you for knowing everything, holding everything, and never
making me feel like *too much*. You were my ground crew when I
couldn't lift off—and you never asked for credit.
This is me giving it.

TO CHARLES—

You arrived like a plot twist I didn't see coming.
Right when I was unraveling, you stayed.
You kept showing up.
You made love feel less like a performance, and more like home.
That kind of love rewired me.

TO GRETCHEN—

For holding it down through the glorious, the gritty, and the weird.
For the *is this cute or crazy?* calls, the fun shoots, the fierce photos,
and the friendship that stayed solid.
Only we know the real behind the scenes—and I'm keeping it that way.

TO MY TRIBE—

You knew exactly when to drop a snack, a meme, a hug, or a full-blown
emotional rescue mission.
You showed up—quietly, loudly, and always right on time.
You're the real ride-or-dies.

TO ALICE—

You taught me the craft, how to see story.
You helped me find courage, put my voice on the page.
Through treatment and spirals, you held the line
and always circled back to the truth.

Those lessons live here, too—
we wrote a show, we followed the crane.
I'm still following—maybe the crane,
or just something crane-shaped in the distance.

TO THE HEALERS, HELPERS, NEEDLE-POKERS, AND TRUTH-TELLERS—

Thank you for stabbing me gently, speaking truth boldly, and holding
the line when I tried to ghost my own healing.

TO MY PAST SELF—

You did your best.
You performed, created, and got back up—every time.
You didn't know what was coming.
But you kept going.

I'm not you anymore—
but I wouldn't be me without you.

Taira 2.0 is here now.
Stronger. Softer.
A little weirder.
Finally home.

TO ANYONE WHO'S EVER FELT BROKEN,
BALD, BRUISED, OR A LITTLE LOST—
I see you.
Keep going.

AND TO LIFE—MESSY, MAGICAL,
RUTHLESS, RADIANT LIFE—
Thank you for the plot twists.
Even the ones that left me *a little buzzed.*

about the author

Taira Soo is a writer, creative, and chronic shapeshifter.
Dancer, designer, business owner, cancer patient—
walking contradiction, sometimes all in the same week.

She lives in Los Angeles with her dog, Kenzi,
who moonlights as both emotional support animal and low-key cult
leader.

This is her first book.
It wasn't planned. It wasn't polished.
But it was necessary.

Written from the messy middle—before things were tied in a bow.
She hopes it meets you wherever you are.

Probably not her last.
(Something's always humming.)

about the dog

Kenzi is a part-time emotional support animal, full-time emotional support *menace.*

She specializes in silent judgment, dramatic sighs, and knowing exactly when to curl up beside you.

She's never technically run a cult. But if she did—you'd join.

(Kenzi approved this message.)

Meet the Real Kenzi
Yes, she's judging you.
Always has been.

Silent judgment is her love language.